AMERICAN
WAR LIBRARY

★ ★ ★ ★

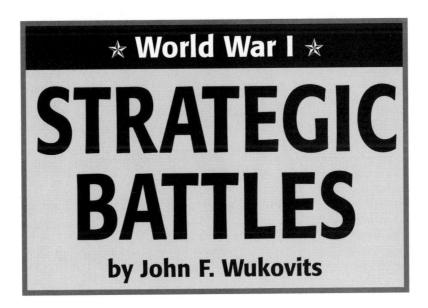

★ World War I ★

STRATEGIC BATTLES

by John F. Wukovits

Lucent Books, 10911 Technology Place, San Diego, CA 92197

Titles in The American War Library series include:

World War II
Hitler and the Nazis
Kamikazes
Leaders and Generals
Life as a POW
Life of an American Soldier in
  Europe
Strategic Battles in Europe
Strategic Battles in the Pacific
The War at Home
Weapons of War

The Civil War
Leaders of the North and South
Life Among the Soldiers and
  Cavalry
Lincoln and the Abolition of
  Slavery
Strategic Battles
Weapons of War

Library of Congress Cataloging-in-Publication Data

Wukovits, John F., 1944–
   Strategic battles / by John F. Wukovits
      p. cm. — (American war library. World War I)
Includes bibliographical references and index.
Summary: Describes the campaigns and battles on land and in the air
during World War I.
   ISBN 1-56006-836-1 (alk. paper)
   1. World War, 1914–1918—Campaigns—Juvenile literature. 2. Battles—
History—20th century—Juvenile literature. I. Title. II. Series.
   D521.W77 2002
   940.4'1—dc21

                                                    2001003018

Printed in the U.S.A.

★ Contents ★

A Nation Forged by War

The United States, like many nations, was forged and defined by war. Despite Benjamin Franklin's opinion that "There never was a good war or a bad peace," the United States owes its very existence to the War of Independence, one to which Franklin wholeheartedly subscribed. The country forged by war in 1776 was tempered and made stronger by the Civil War in the 1860s.

The Texas Revolution, the Mexican-American War, and the Spanish-American War expanded the country's borders and gave it overseas possessions. These wars made the United States a world power, but this status came with a price, as the nation became a key but reluctant player in both World War I and World War II.

Each successive war further defined the country's role on the world stage. Following World War II, U.S. foreign policy redefined itself to focus on the role of defender, not only of the freedom of its own citizens, but also of the freedom of people everywhere. During the cold war that followed World War II until the collapse of the Soviet Union, defending the world meant fighting communism. This goal, manifested in the Korean and Vietnam conflicts, proved elusive, and soured the American public on its achievability. As the United States emerged as the world's sole superpower, American foreign policy has been guided less by national interest and more on protecting international human rights. But as involvement in Somalia and Kosovo prove, this goal has been equally elusive.

As a result, the country's view of itself changed. Bolstered by victories in World Wars I and II, Americans first relished the role of protector. But, as war followed war in a seemingly endless procession, Americans began to doubt their leaders, their motives, and themselves. The Vietnam War especially caused people to question the validity of sending its young people to die in places where they were not particularly wanted and for people who did not seem especially grateful.

While the most obvious changes brought about by America's wars have been geopolitical in nature, many other aspects of society have been touched. War often does not bring about change directly, but acts instead like the catalyst in a chemical reaction, accelerating changes already in progress.

Some of these changes have been societal. The role of women in the United States had been slowly changing, but World War II put thousands into the workforce and into uniform. They might have gone back to being housewives after the war, but equality, once experienced, would not be forgotten.

Likewise, wars have accelerated technological change. The necessity for faster airplanes and a more destructive bomb led to the development of jet planes and nuclear energy. Artificial fibers developed for parachutes in the 1940s were used in the clothing of the 1950s.

Lucent Books' American War Library covers key wars in the development of the nation. Each war is covered in several volumes, to allow for more detail, context, and to provide volumes on often neglected subjects, such as the kamikazes of World War II, or weapons used in the Civil War. As with all Lucent Books, notes, annotated bibliographies, and appendixes such as glossaries give students a launching point for further research. In addition, sidebars and archival photographs enhance the text. Together, each volume in The American War Library will aid students in understanding how America's wars have shaped and changed its politics, economics, and society.

"Don't Do It Again"

Oon June 28, 1914, Archduke Franz Ferdinand, the heir to the Austrian throne, and his wife Sophie happily waved to the crowds as their automobile transported them through the streets of Sarajevo, the capital city of Bosnia. Their happiness, and with it that of much of the Western world, abruptly ended when a teenage assassin named Gavrilo Princip, a member of a group devoted to Serbian freedom from Austro-Hungarian rule, stepped from the curb and fired into the passing car.

The murders of the royal couple dragged Europe into four years of horror. When Austria-Hungary declared war against Serbia, other major nations, bound by treaty obligations, rushed to the support of their allies, and within weeks two warring camps prepared for hostilities. The Allies on the one side, dominated by France, Russia, and Great Britain, braced for confrontation with the Central Powers on the other, headed by Germany and Austria-Hungary.

Most of Europe's youth enthusiastically joined their country's military. Citizens in Paris, France, cried out "To Berlin!" and whenever groups of soldiers passed by on their way to train stations young women shoved flowers into the soldiers' guns and kissed them. An equally volatile crowd, including a young unemployed painter named

The assassinations of Archduke Ferdinand (right) and his wife Sophie triggered the onslaught of World War I.

Adolf Hitler, gathered in Munich, Germany, to cheer the news of war. Everyone on both sides expected a speedy victory.

Within months the jubilation disappeared as young men learned that warfare, while initially appearing festive and exciting, offered little but bloodshed and death. Europe's next generation placed its faith in the top military officials to lead them to triumph on the battlefield, but instead of inventive plans to defeat the opponent, soldiers were sent en masse to overcome their enemy by shear numbers, a holdover of nineteenth-century military strategy. Unfortunately, in the modern age of artillery and the machine gun, the brave and willing were simply slaughtered. Four long years of strife, consisting of battles that unfolded in the same monotonous manner time after time, gripped the continent and drained the youth from all major combatants.

Few military officials grasped the futility of sending men in uniforms to fight against modern weapons. Bodies accumulated in astonishing numbers, but still the generals relied on the same strategy—line up the men in an impressive-looking array and order them to cross open fields while under heavy fire.

The predictable results stunned observers. Casualty figures for a single day's combat surpassed totals previously recorded for entire campaigns or even wars. At Belleau Wood, for instance, the U.S. Marines lost more men in one day than it had in its entire history.

Yet few military leaders heeded the lesson. Winston Churchill, the famed British leader of the next world war, attended a lecture on January 17, 1916, in which the speaker outlined the strategy used in the recent Battle of Loos, which took many lives. After the speech, Churchill wrote his wife that while most in the audience courteously listened, few heard the message.

> The theater was crowded with generals and officers. [The speaker] spoke very well but his tale was one of hopeless failure, of sublime heroism utterly wasted and of splendid Scottish soldiers shorn away in vain with never the ghost of a chance of success. 6,000 killed and wounded out of 10,000 in this Scottish division alone. Alas, alas. Afterwards they asked what was the lesson of the lecture. I restrained an impulse to reply "Don't do it again." But they will—I have no doubt.[1]

They did, and consequently the losses for the war set ghastly records. An average of five thousand six hundred soldiers were killed for each day of the four-year war, while 8 million soldiers died fighting for their nations. Hundreds of thousands more suffered from crippling wounds and psychological disorders.

Incredible Arrogance and Heart-Lifting Valor

The battles selected for this book represent the pattern of combat that prevailed in World

War I. They provide a glimpse into the senseless slaughter, but they also present the military remedies that, if followed, could have avoided much of the death. The chapters contain incredible arrogance and refusal to change by some military commanders, but also deliver stories of heart-lifting heroism and valor.

Even though armies clashed in Russia and the Middle East, six of the featured battles occurred on the western front in

The number of casualties rose dramatically as traditional combat strategies proved to be futile against modern artillery.

France. Because this volume forms a portion of the American War Library series, operations involving the U.S. Army and Marines dominate—and those unfolded on the western front. By the time of the United States' entrance into the war in

1917, fighting had halted on the eastern front with Russia's removal from the war, and while not easily dismissed, operations in the Middle East rarely rivaled the western front in importance. One Middle Eastern battle, the fighting in the Dardanelles, is included, but the main focus rests with the western front.

The first chapter depicts the German drive through Belgium into France and shows how the hopes for a quick war were shattered at the walls of Belgian forts. Instead of racing into Paris and victory, Germany stalled and stumbled, thereby permitting France, Great Britain, and Russia time to organize. The stage had been set in the conflict's opening days for a protracted war that offered the stark realities of trench warfare.

Great Britain hoped to break the stalemate in the trenches along the western front by staging an invasion in the Dardanelles Strait in Turkey. This effort, too, dissolved into more of the same, with soldiers stepping in unison toward their enemy and being cut down by the thousands. Rather than find a solution to the trenches, the Dardanelles campaign became simply one more example of unimaginative military thinking.

The third battle, at Verdun, was one of the war's more stirring stories. Bolstered by the effective leadership of General Henri Philippe Pétain, the French turned aside a larger German attacking force around the

Few military commanders grasped the destructive potential of the German tank.

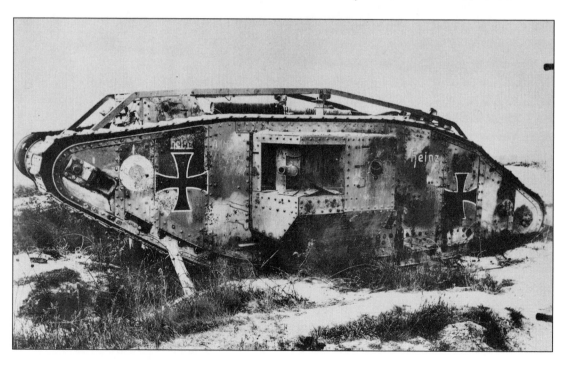

venerable city of Verdun. Months of combat produced a moral victory for the French that won world admiration, but also tallied close to 1 million casualties.

Fighting at the Somme, the fourth battle selected, was one of the more shocking examples of human slaughter, while also providing a solution to trench warfare with the initial appearance of the tank. Sadly, few military commanders grasped the new weapon's potential until the next world war.

The final three chapters represent battles fought mainly by American soldiers. Their initiation in a dense plot of land called Belleau Wood proved that the men from overseas could fight on an equal basis with the enemy. Their drive against Saint-Mihiel offered the Americans a chance to fight as a unit under its own command and handed the world its first glimpse of a major offensive through the air, and the fighting in the Meuse-Argonne ended the hostilities.

Four years after war commenced, the European combatants gazed at each other across battle lines that had hardly altered in the intervening months. Little had been accomplished except to blacken French forests and churn French soil. The hatred and bit-

The Allies and the Central Powers

The war split Europe into two factions—the Allies and the Central Powers. The major nations on each side were:

Allies
Austria
Belgium
Canada
France
Great Britain
Greece
New Zealand
Russia
United States

Central Powers
Austria-Hungary
Bulgaria
Germany
Ottoman Empire (Turkey)

terness produced by World War I simmered for twenty-one years, when a second, and more immense, slaughter opened with World War II.

Chapter 1

The Drive Toward Paris

Confidence usually dominates on the day before a campaign. Generals have convinced themselves that their elaborate strategies cannot possibly fail, and soldiers have been told that only a physically and morally inferior foe stands between them and triumph. Quite often, though, as occurred along the Belgian-French border in 1914, reality quickly fell short of expectations.

False Optimism

German military leaders trumpeted their invasion plans of France as unbeatable. Knowing that in the wake of the brutal Franco-Prussian War of 1871 France constructed an elaborate complex of forts facing the German border, German strategists devised an attack plan that undermined the enemy's advantage. Instead of charging directly against these strongholds, the Germans chose to simply avoid them by shifting the focus of attack north. Masses of German soldiers would smash through Bel-

gium into France, then swerve to the east to attack French armies along the border.

Although tactically prudent, the plan's flaw lay in its tight timetable. The Germans had to break through Belgium and invade France before the French Army had time to mobilize and before the Russians could field an army on Germany's eastern border. To advance beyond Belgium, though, the Germans had to neutralize a series of Belgian forts, especially around the town of Liège, where twelve forts built on high ground—six along either side of the Meuse River— peered menacingly down at the avenue of advance. Once the Germans raced through those forts, open plains offered a speedy route into the heart of France. If the German attack faltered to any degree, their opponents would have time to mount a stronger defense and turn what many had expected to be a fast war into a lengthy conflict.

At first, France fashioned its military plans on the premise that Germany would attack directly across the shared border into

France, as the nation did in 1871. A string of forts thus protected that border from a German invasion. By 1914, though, French strategy shifted to the offensive. General Joseph Joffre, the French commander in chief, correctly assumed the Germans would attack through Belgium, the same route that had been used by travelers for hundreds of years to quickly reach Paris. While the enemy was speeding along that avenue, Joffre planned to launch his own invasion across the border with Germany, shove the German defenders against the Rhine River, then swing north to sever the lines of communications with the forces fighting in Belgium. This strategy would

bring the German operation to a halt and end the war in France's favor. Like the Germans, Joffre felt confident that his men, buttressed by a unit of British soldiers who would come across the channel from England, could handily defeat the enemy.

The Belgian government suffered from the same sort of delusional thinking. More than eighty thousand soldiers stood between Liège and the nation's capital, Brussels, most stationed in one of the many bastions constructed to hold off the Germans until help arrived from France and England. The forts housed four hundred guns, including mammoth cannons hurling shells eight inches in diameter, and machine

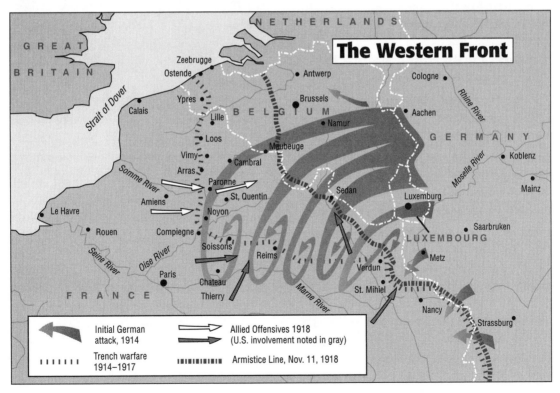

guns. The concrete fortifications, designed to withstand fire from opposing eight-inch shells, contained gun turrets in every corner to establish a crossfire on advancing soldiers, thirty-foot-deep dry moats, and searchlights to prevent a surprise nighttime attack.

False optimism thus gripped European military leaders as the initial conflicts of the war dawned in August 1914. The Belgians counted on their forts holdings off the Germans; the French believed its army could swing into Germany and defeat the enemy; the Germans counted on their highly trained forces to crush Belgian resistance and trap French armies inside France. Each side believed the fighting would be brief and victorious. None was correct.

"You Will Be Home Before the Leaves Have Fallen"

The ordinary foot soldier fell into the same erroneous thinking. With unit banners flying and locals cheering, German soldiers gathered in their assigned positions for the August 4 assault. One observer wrote, "The Germans left with the light of victory already in their eyes, one of the most truculent being [one officer] . . . who promised to send a post card from Paris in a few weeks!"[2]

Even the German ruler Kaiser Wilhelm traveled to the starting lines to encourage his men. "You will be home before the leaves have fallen from the trees,"[3] he promised.

Heady with this dangerous optimism, German troops advanced in the militarily accepted fashion of neat rows across the border

Kaiser Wilhelm II, the emperor of Germany during World War I, and other military leaders truly believed the fighting would not last long.

into Belgium toward Liège, where murderous Belgian machine gun fire from nearby forts cut them to shreds. Hundreds of Germans fell; corpses piled up waist high in some spots. The hapless German soldiers were the first of World War I to experience one of the war's harshest lessons—that soldiers marching into battle according to time-honored customs were no match for modern weapons. It was a lesson that would be endlessly repeated in Europe with tragic results.

The Belgian commander at Liège, General Gerard Leman, received orders to defend the town. The vibrant officer organized such a successful effort that he delayed the German drive for ten days, a feat which handed the French and British governments time to organize their forces.

To repulse the German soldiers from their soil, Belgian citizens grabbed rifles and shot at the enemy from hidden positions in fields, behind trees, and from buildings. Already flustered that their advance had been slowed by the Belgian forts, irate German commanders retaliated with a vengeance that stunned the world.

When sniper fire came from the Belgian town of Herve, German soldiers destroyed almost every building. A German journalist accompanied the soldiers and reported that of five hundred homes, "only nineteen remain. Corpses are lying all over the place; everywhere there is a smell of burning. The church is a broken heap of ruins."[4]

In another village, the Germans shot 612 men, women, and children as retribution, including a three-week-old baby being held by its mother. The Belgian government tried to discourage civilian fighting, but

---

Herve church was one of the many buildings destroyed by the Germans after Belgian snipers had sabotaged German troops.

found it difficult to dissuade people whose homes and livelihoods were threatened. A familiar, yet tragic, scene all too common in war dominated the Belgian countryside as thousands of refugees poured out of burning cities and fled to the countryside, carrying what few precious items they could.

World leaders heaped condemnation on the Germans, who justified their actions by claiming they had to protect their own men. German chief of staff Helmuth von Moltke admitted "Our advance in Belgium is certainly brutal, but we are fighting for our lives and all who get in the way must take the consequences."[5]

Another German official, Baron von Stumm, said in exasperation, "Oh, the poor fools! Why don't they get out of the way of the steam roller? We don't want to hurt them, but if they stand in our way they will be ground into the dirt."[6]

The Germans haphazardly moved forward until they introduced a weapon that could answer the machine gun—concentrated artillery fire. Mammoth guns nicknamed "Big Berthas" (after the wife of the man whose factories produced the guns) hurled a 16.5-inch, one-ton shell nine miles with such impact that a small number of guns could handily demolish a Belgian fortress. The first of the twelve forts fell under a thunderous barrage on August 10,

Capable of lobbing shells a distance of nine miles, large guns nicknamed "Big Berthas" easily demolished forts in Belgium.

and within six days ten more forts succumbed to Big Bertha's frightening power.

Liège withstood the German pounding for ten days before the town capitulated. Though eventually their resistance gave out, the Belgians slowed the German drive enough to give France and England more time to prepare on the west, and Russia on the east. This, in turn, led to a victory a few weeks later in front of Paris that might not have occurred without the heroic Belgian stand.

The first German soldiers stepped into Brussels, the Belgian capital, on August 20. Despite the mauling administered by Belgian machine guns, the Germans were in relatively good shape. Though advancing slower than expected, two armies had pushed one hundred miles beyond the German border in less than three weeks, and now posed threats to the interior of France and port cities to the north. French troops stirred against German units elsewhere, and British troops landed on the continent, but German officers dismissed both as nuisances to be swept aside.

Initial Success

While the German Army ravaged Belgium, the French Army embarked upon its own offensive into Germany. Joffre intended to retake the provinces of Alsace-Lorraine, seized by Germany in 1870, then shove the German forces back to the Rhine before swerving north to hit Moltke's army in Belgium from the rear. Poor French preparation and inadequate reconnaissance, in part because of an

Frightening New War

One of the newer methods of warfare that appeared in World War I was the massed artillery barrage, whereby large numbers of big guns blanketed an area with its thunderous fire. The tactic was a nightmare that no one who survived would forget. In his book, *The First World War*, historian Martin Gilbert presents the thoughts of British captain Edward L. Spears after he witnessed the first of what would be many such episodes.

> A dog was barking at some sheep. A girl was singing as she walked down the lane behind us. From a little farm away on the right came the voices of laughter of some soldiers cooking their evening meal. Darkness grew in the far distance as the light began to fail. Then, without a moment's warning, with a suddenness that made us start and strain our eyes to see what our minds could not realise, we saw the whole horizon burst into flame.

arrogant attitude that dismissed the Germans as inferior, led to disaster for Joffre.

French forces headed into Germany on August 4, just as Moltke's troops entered Belgium. Initial gains heartened the French, who were unaware that the enemy was purposely drawing them deeper into Germany as a preliminary to a potent counterattack. By August 19 the French had sprinted to the villages of Zillisheim and Flaxanden ten miles from the Rhine, but they were to advance no farther.

Two reasons caused the halt. First, Joffre had to slow his advance because the fighting in Belgium required more attention. Second, a massive German counterattack smashed into French lines on August 20.

French forces tried to stem the rush, but imitating the German soldiers in Belgium, they marched in splendidly organized lines directly into withering German machine gun fire. Overconfident French troops headed toward the enemy without even carrying hand grenades, positive they could defeat their foe with rifle and bayonet. German machine gun fire put an abrupt end to their wishful thinking by dropping thousands of French troops before they closed the distance.

One French platoon commander led his men toward a bridge when a bullet shattered his knee. Within seconds, another soldier's body slumped on top of the fallen lieutenant, who lay on the ground listening to "the dull thud of bullets entering the bodies of the dead and wounded that lay about."[7] Calling on his inner strength, the officer dragged himself to safety and was taken to a hospital. Lieutenant Charles de Gaulle, future French president, recovered to fight again.

All along the front, French and Belgian troops fled the victorious Germans and battled with refugees for access to roads. The August 12 arrival of 120,000 British troops bolstered morale, but the sorry plight of their allies sobered the British as they hastened to Mons to stop the Germans. Captain Edward L. Spears watched a seemingly endless stream of refugees and later wrote:

A grey mob, grey because the black clothes most of them wore were covered with dust, was filing by; they occupied the whole width of the road, going in absolute silence, the only sound being that of very tired feet dragging. Each individual in that slowly-moving mass looked the embodiment of a personal tragedy; men and women with set staring faces, carrying heavy bundles, moving on they knew not where, formed a background of grim despair.[8]

The British moved into position at Mons and waited for the inevitable German attack. On August 22 General Heinrich von Kluck's First Army opened with a cavalry charge, which was as criminally futile against machine guns as was a straightforward troop advancement. Horses and riders fell in unison, their life's blood intermingling in the dusty soil. German infantry followed and added their bodies to those recently slain.

"Their losses were very heavy," explained British general Horace Smith-Dorrien, "for they came on in dense formations, offering the most perfect targets, and it was not until they had been mown down in thousands that they adopted more open formations."[9]

In what was becoming an ominous foreshadow of the fighting that would typify World War I combat, murderous machine gun fire was checked by more destructive artillery bombardments. German artillery gradually reduced British opposition and forced the weary men to fall back in a five-day-long retreat. The British lost more than four thousand men at Mons, but like the Belgians earlier, they slowed the German drive into France.

Still, Moltke's armies stood on French territory. Once across the border, the Germans headed south toward the Marne River and Paris, routing the French at the Sambre River and trapping the British at Le Cateau. With the Germans close behind, on August 25 British general Smith-Dorrien discussed with his staff the two choices they faced: continued retreat or battle. After listening to each man's opinion, Smith-Dorrien said, "Very well, gentlemen, we will fight."[10]

The Germans attacked Smith-Dorrien's lines at daylight on August 26 and, while the British fought valiantly from behind stone walls and trees, they were no match for the enemy artillery. After losing more than eight thousand men, Smith-Dorrien ordered a further retreat.

British and French attempts to hold Germany dissolved all along the front. In ten days, for instance, the French Army lost three hundred thousand soldiers. Units retreated as quickly as they could, and on September 2 the French government fled Paris for Bordeaux. One million French citizens gathered belongings and abandoned the French capital, and in some spots French soldiers retreated in such disorder that officers

German soldiers manning a machine gun emplacement prepare to fire on advancing French troops.

Retreat

In the opening weeks of war, the British and French armies executed a relatively organized withdrawal from Belgium into France. The men lived to fight on and eventually reverse the course of battle, but during the retreat they more closely resembled spectral figures rather than a proud fighting force. In his history, *The First World War*, Martin Gilbert includes the comment of a British officer, Captain Edward L. Spears, about the retreat of the French Army. Spears also refers to the suffering of innocent animals.

Heads down, red trousers and blue coats indistinguishable for dust, bumping into transport, into abandoned carts, into each other, they shuffled down the endless roads, their eyes filled with dust that dimmed the scalding landscape, so that they saw clearly only the foreground of discarded packs, prostrate men, and an occasional abandoned gun. Dead and dying horses that had dropped from their tracks in fatigue, lay in great numbers by the side of the roads. Worse still, horses dying but not yet dead, sometimes struggling a little, a strange appeal in their eyes, looked at the passing columns whose dust covered them, caking their thirsty lips and nostrils.

shot into their own men in attempts to halt the mad rush.

Disaster loomed for the Allies. Should Paris fall, France would succumb and England would be isolated on its island. Moltke, learning that citizens fled Paris, expected that the fighting would soon be over.

The German officer's optimism was premature, as three factors combined to spoil his dream. First, the farther the Germans moved into France, the harder it became for supply units to move equipment to the front, while it became easier to reinforce the French and British, whose lines of supply shortened. Second, Moltke and other Germans had not counted on the will of the French people to defend their capital. Third, even fate took a hand when a German officer driving to headquarters took a wrong turn in the road and headed into a French patrol. The French killed the officer, then retrieved from his body a map marking the disposition of Ger-man troops and papers indicating that the German forces, instead of swinging beyond Paris to surround the capital, had veered to the southeast. This handed an enterprising French officer, General Joseph Gallieni, the opportunity to launch the counterattack that altered the battle's outcome.

"I Shall Carry Out to the End"

With the French capital threatened, Joffre rushed reinforcements from other regions. He stripped the Franco-German border of all but essential forces and called on soldiers to fight for the honor of France. On August 26 Gallieni, a brilliant motivator and military leader, assumed command of Paris's defense. He rallied the city's inhabitants by saying, "I have received a mandate to defend Paris against the invader. This mandate I shall carry out to the end."[11] The energetic Gallieni ordered the construction of a line of trenches and barricades to protect the city and brought in hundreds of farm animals from surrounding fields to feed the populace.

Moltke's optimism aided Gallieni's cause by weakening the German attackers. Believing the French were defeated, on August 25 Moltke pulled some troops out of the fighting in France for transfer to the Russian front. He saw no reason to be concerned over the French defenders in Paris, and he even started plans for a victory celebration. Triumph appeared hours away on September 3 when German forces moved within eight miles of the city, and German propaganda leaflets rained down on Paris proclaiming all hope was gone. Frantic French citizens jammed train stations in an effort to leave the threatened capital.

Then came what the French call the "Miracle of the Marne," which started when von Kluck's units raced to the east of Paris. This new axis of advance created a twenty-mile gap between German armies and offered Gallieni the opportunity to strike into the opening against the enemy right flank. "I dare not believe it," cried Gallieni. "It is too good to be true."[12]

The excited general gathered every soldier he could find, then organized a vast fleet of seven hundred Paris taxicabs and automobiles to shuttle them to the front. He asked every citizen with a vehicle to volunteer for duty, and ordered the police to halt taxicabs, even those filled with civilian passengers, and commandeer them for military use. Joffre added inspiration by exhorting his men, "At the moment when the battle upon which hangs the fate of France is about to begin, all must remember that the time for looking back is past; every effort must be concentrated on attacking and throwing the enemy back." Joffre added that the men

French soldiers (pictured) fight in Paris in "the Miracle of the Marne," the battle that turned back the Germans.

"must die where they stand rather than give way."[13]

On September 5, with the Germans within view of the Eiffel Tower, the French opened a seven-day battle to Paris's northeast. Hundreds of small engagements pitted French valor against German bravery, machine guns against trenches, artillery shells against barricades. The weary Germans, who had been advancing for thirty-three consecutive days, proved a gallant adversary, but the stout French, battling for their lives and country, turned the tide. Opposing militants killed from a distance with rifles, then moved in close to kill with bayonets and bare hands.

Stories illustrate the fighting. In the marshes of Saint Gond, General Ferdinand Foch's men held off swarms of attacking Germans in bloody bayonet battles. With bodies piling around his position and the Germans rushing on three sides, Foch supposedly said, "My flanks are turned; my center gives way; I attack!"[14] Whether he uttered the phrase or not, the sentiment typified the French spirit in Paris.

In another action a French captain led a suicidal charge into German machine guns. Bullets cut him down before he moved fifty yards. Lieutenant Charles de la Cornilliere took his place, guided the troops for a few minutes, then slumped to the ground with mortal wounds of his own. A sergeant rushed to his aid, but he, too, was killed by German fire. When the remaining men started to panic, the dying Cornilliere struggled to his knees and shouted, "Yes, the lieutenant has been killed, but keep on firm!"[15] Emboldened by their dying officer's courage, the French soldiers stood their ground and turned back the Germans.

Gradually the Germans, surprised by the effectiveness of the French defense and petrified that their carefully laid plans stood in shreds, showed signs of disorganization. One staff officer wrote of Moltke and the other top leaders, "Desperate panic seized severely the entire army, or to be more correct, the greater part of the leaders. Moltke completely collapsed. He sat with a pallid face gazing at the map, dead to all feeling, a broken man."[16]

"Some Horrible Thing Was Advancing to Grip Us"

With one hundred thousand British soldiers nearing Paris to help the embattled French, on September 11 the Germans pulled back to high ground along the Aisne River to the north. They dug trenches, set machine guns, and strung barbed wire along the front.

A series of encounters ensued as each side tried to swing around the other side's northern flank. As one combatant edged north, the other did likewise to block the attempt. The opposing armies engaged in a gruesome ballet in which they gradually stretched the lines and added hundreds of miles to the existing trenches. The macabre dance only halted when they reached the coastline bordering the English Channel. By the end of September two sets of trench lines dissected the French countryside from

Switzerland in the south to the Belgian coast in the north, ushering in a period of stalemate along the western front in which armies marched to their deaths in a new, terrifying style of battle in the trenches and the land between them.

The German and French military each suffered more than 250,000 casualties in this opening phase of the war. When the guns quieted, the German gamble to roll up opposition in the west had failed, and with it its hopes for a speedy war. In its place came a protracted war of machine guns and artillery, mass slaughter and misery.

Moltke sensed the disturbing change. On September 12 he wrote his wife,

> Things are going badly. The battles east of Paris are turning against us. The great hopes that the beginning of the war gave us have been dashed. We shall finally wear ourselves out in this struggle on two fronts! What a difference from the brilliant beginning of our campaign! Now it is cruel disillusion. And we must pay for all this devastation. [17]

Moltke's prophetic words came true when he was replaced as supreme German com-

A wounded soldier falls victim to trench warfare, a new style of combat that squelched hopes of a speedy war.

mander by Erich von Falkenhayn, the former Prussian minister of war.

Sitting in the trenches, British officer Captain Edward L. Spears also sensed a difference. His forebodings had more to do with the murderous fashion of warfare about to be introduced to Europe, though. Spears wrote,

> A chill of horror came over us. War seemed suddenly to have assumed a merciless, ruthless aspect that we had not realized till then. Hitherto it had been war as we had conceived it, hard blows, straight dealing, but now for the first time we felt as if some horrible Thing, utterly merciless, was advancing to grip us.[18]

Chapter 2

Gallipoli

With Germany's gamble failing to achieve a quick end to the war, both sides settled into the misery that became trench warfare. Death and destruction dominated the battlefields of the western front, not for a day or week, but for a mind-numbing succession of months that sent casualties soaring. Military and political leaders feared that unless an alternative to trench warfare was found, Europe's youth would bleed to death in France's rolling farmlands.

Solution in the Dardanelles

Allied leaders turned to the Dardanelles for the answer. The Dardanelles Strait separates Europe from Asia and splits Turkey into two portions, European Turkey and Asian Turkey. Because the strait provides a water route from the Black Sea to the Aegean Sea, it has long been an important location for military reasons. Fifteen major battles have been fought in the region, including one in A.D. 378 in which the Goths killed the Roman emperor Valens and helped usher in the downfall of Rome.

The strait is bounded to the north by the Gallipoli Peninsula. Sixty miles long and ranging from four to thirteen miles wide, the peninsula forms the southern portion of European Turkey. A foreboding land consisting mainly of rocky terrain, the peninsula featured but one dirt road running along its length. The rest of the barren land offered little but challenges to anyone desiring to use it, whether it be a farmer or a soldier. Lofty ridges and steep slopes overlook the beaches, providing excellent defensive positions for an army to repulse an invasion.

Yet this is precisely where the Allies determined to strike. Mainly at the suggestion of British politician Winston Churchill, the Allies hoped to crack the stalemate existing in Europe, halt the carnage that ensued, assist Russia by diverting Turkish attention from the Russian front, and ultimately knock Turkey out of the war.

To mount a successful campaign in such an ominous location required sufficient manpower and imaginative planning, but the Allies lacked both. They first considered a land campaign, then a naval assault, then a combined land-sea offensive. Finally, they settled upon an attempt by the British and French navies to dash through the straits and destroy Turkish fortifications along the way. Should that fail, then a land campaign would be executed.

On March 18, 1915, Allied warships inched into the straits, not knowing if they would be fired upon by Turkish guns in shoreline forts. As it turned out, that was the

A memorial in Gallipoli commemorates the battle that took place between Allied and Turkish forces in March 1915.

least of their worries. The stillness was shattered when the French battleship *Bouvet* suddenly exploded, rolled over, and sank in minutes, taking seven hundred French sailors to watery graves. The squadron of ships ran into a string of mines that the Turks had planted in the narrows. In rapid order another mine hit the British battle cruiser *Inflexible* and forced the ship to retire, and others struck and sank the two

British battleships, *Irresistible* and *Ocean*. The remainder of the squadron withdrew to safety, but Allied commanders had been handed an emphatic lesson: Only a land campaign could wrest control of the region from Turkey. Turkey, though, had been forewarned of the Allied interest in the Dardanelles; Turkey used the lull between the naval action and the arrival of Allied soldiers to strengthen the area's defenses.

Fatal Assumptions

The British officer in command of the land expedition, General Sir Ian Hamilton, committed the first in a disastrous series of blunders that doomed the Gallipoli attack before it started. He knew little of the ter-

rain at Gallipoli; instead of waiting until his staff could deliver a militarily sound description of the peninsula and the Turkish forces standing watch, he relied on tourist manuals and maps hastily purchased in London bookstores. When Hamilton left England, he had not even selected the landing sites for his troops.

As the ships steamed through the Mediterranean Sea, Hamilton finalized the plans for his eighty-five thousand men. To divert attention from the main landing beaches, a French division would land at

The British battleship Inflexible *was hit by a mine that forced the cruiser to pull out of the fighting in Gallipoli.*

Kum Kale on the Asiatic shore across from Gallipoli, and the Royal Naval Division would head north to hit Bulair at the peninsula's top portion. The Australian–New Zealand Army Corps, called Anzacs, would crash ashore twelve miles above the peninsula's southern tip at a location labeled Anzac Cove, rush across to the eastern side, and attack Turkish troops from behind. Meanwhile, the British 29th Division would hit in five spots at Cape Helles on the peninsula's extreme southern tip and head to high ground immediately beyond.

Unfortunately for the Allies, Hamilton needed more men if he were to storm the Turkish forces at five different spots, but the Allied leader assumed the Turks would react in confusion and fail to organize a counterattack until his units were already

Foolish Attitude

World War I contained numerous examples of the rigid mindset that paralyzed military commanders and led to continued slaughter. One such notion was that individual valor and spirit could overcome guns and barbed wire, and that the British soldier is superior to the fighting men of any other nation. In his book, *A Short History of World War I*, historian James L. Stokesbury includes a quote by General Sir Ian Hamilton to illustrate such folly:

Let me bring my lads face to face with the Turks in the open field, we *must* beat them every time because British volunteer soldiers are superior individuals to Anatolians, Syrians, or Arabs and are animated with a superior ideal and equal joy in battle.

entrenched ashore. This assumption would cost men their lives.

They sailed in blissful ignorance, however, as the force departed from its final collection spot in Egypt and headed toward Gallipoli. Military bands played martial tunes and crowds lined the shores to cheer as the squadron steamed away. Allied leaders, blinded by optimism, expected an easy victory over what they considered as the inferior Turks.

Those Turks had a surprise in store. Short of the necessary manpower to adequately defend the entire peninsula— about eighty-four thousand soldiers to guard 150 miles of coastline—the German officer in command of the Turkish forces, General Liman von Sanders, relied on nature as his ally. Since most of the peninsula consisted of ragged cliffs that dominated the beaches, he scattered his men along the crests of ridges at likely landing spots. Machine gun nests guarded the approaches, and patrols continually scoured the coast for signs of imminent action. Sanders strung miles of barbed wire in the only area offering a level beach, at Bulair, toward which the Royal Naval Division headed. Because he could not predict where Hamilton's primary thrust would come, Sanders stationed his main force in the peninsula's midsection until the Allies landed, at which time he planned to rush reinforcements to the most endangered location.

The first Allied soldiers streamed ashore on April 25, 1915. The French handily shoved aside meager Turkish resistance

When the French landed at Anzac Cove (pictured) they swiftly broke through the weaker Turkish force that was waiting for them.

at Kum Kale, and the Royal Naval Division so quickly landed at Bulair that Sanders had to divert reinforcements to the region. If the other beaches experienced similar conditions, the Allies could expect complete success. It was not to be.

"How We Longed for Nightfall!"

The Australian and New Zealand troops suffered first. Known for their superb training and excellent physical condition, the Anzacs carried an impeccable reputation into battle. Each man started military training while still in school, and few shirked their patriotic responsibility. One soldier stated that when the call for fighting men went out, "University classes emptied, sports fixtures were abandoned. To be left behind was unthinkable. If your mate was going, then somehow you had to get away too." [19]

Two hundred troop transports inched toward Anzac Cove in the early morning light on April 25. The men quietly stepped from the transports into rowboats, which were then tugged through heavy currents

Courageous Kemal

One of the most remarkable leaders during World War I was Turkey's Mustafa Kemal, the man who later gained fame as the founder of modern Turkey. As a military officer he had few peers, and no one who battled at his side doubted the man's bravery. One instance has become legendary. Facing Anzac forces at Anzac Cove, Kemal stood with his men in a trench while Allied artillery shells crept ever closer. Instead of rushing for cover, Kemal calmly lit a cigarette and stood talking as shells exploded nearby. Then, without explanation, the shelling switched to a different location just as it was due to hit Kemal's trench.

Mustafa Kemal is known for his bravery and for creating modern Turkey.

toward shore. The Anzacs landed one mile away from their intended destination because of the swift current, but the fortunate error deposited them on unguarded beaches. Delighted with their easy landing, the Anzacs started to advance toward the heights that towered above.

They never arrived at the crest. A man destined for fame as the founder of modern Turkey, Mustafa Kemal, rushed to the scene to find the handful of Turks in retreat, but he halted them by saying, "One doesn't run away from the enemy." When the men cried that they had little ammunition, he replied, "If you haven't any ammunition, at least you have your bayonets."[20] He launched a successful counterattack that pinned the Anzacs to the slopes and beaches.

Kemal's courage revitalized his men, who stubbornly held the crests until help arrived. The Anzacs, carrying small spades that proved futile against the rocky terrain, had to fight uphill in the open, while Kemal's men fired downward from hidden positions.

Anzacs died where they crouched. Within one day, sixteen thousand Australian and New Zealand troops jammed Anzac Cove, but they had nowhere to go. Turkish bullets and shells systematically swept the ridges, forcing soldiers and officers alike to find protection wherever they could. A private might be in one hastily dug foxhole, only to find a general huddling in the next. Gradually, a long line of wounded stretched from the slopes to the beaches,

British troops paid the price for waiting for orders to move when they eventually tried to seize the inland area of Anzac Cove.

where they awaited evacuation and tried to avoid enemy artillery shells.

That first day at Anzac Cove offered more horror than any soldier anticipated seeing. Waves of Turkish reinforcements climbed over the bodies of fallen comrades to charge at the Anzacs, who answered with a withering fire. Hour after hour, the Anzacs battled the Turks to a standstill. For the survivors, the day left haunting memories.

"There was no rest, no lull while the rotting dead lay all around us" wrote an Australian soldier, "never a pause in the whole of that long day that started at the crack of dawn. How we longed for nightfall! How we prayed for this ghastly day to end! How we yearned for the sight of the first dark shadow!"[21]

Disaster at Cape Helles

To the south of Anzac Cove, British troops encountered a similar dismal first day at two of the five landing spots. At the beaches designated as S Beach, X Beach, and Y Beach, the forces stepped ashore with little difficulty. Problems set in when they failed to swiftly move inland, as their Anzac counterparts had attempted to do. Meager Turkish resistance faced them at the three beaches, and if the British had rushed to the high ground, they could have commanded the entire area. Instead, they inexplicably remained on the beaches, dug in, and made tea. Rather than taking the initiative, they relaxed and waited for orders from incompetent officers that never came. As a result, the men would later have to pay a heavy price in blood to seize land that could have been theirs for the taking on April 25.

The problems on April 25 came at W Beach and V Beach. Heavy Turkish fire tore into the British while they were still one hundred yards from W Beach. So many soldiers packed each boat that many remained sitting in an upright position even after being killed. Some boats dropped off the men while still too far from shore and the soldiers, weighed down with seventy pounds of equipment, drowned.

After enduring this gauntlet of fire, British soldiers then had to rush across beaches rimmed with barbed wire directly into Turkish machine gun fire. Each man stepped out of the landing craft into a sheet of bullets.

One British officer recalled that "the sea behind was absolutely crimson [from blood], and you could hear the groans through the rattle of musketry. A few were firing. I signaled to them to advance. I then perceived they were all hit."[22]

Throughout April 25, 950 British attempted to land at W Beach; less than half succeeded. That half, however, gallantly pushed forward, eliminated the Turkish opposition, and settled in for an uneasy night.

The British faced only four Turkish machine guns at the nearby V Beach, but the guns inflicted a gruesome carnage that topped W Beach. The British poured out of an older ship, the *River Clyde*, which was run near shore; they stumbled into the water suffering from multiple bullet wounds. One

Twenty thousand British soldiers lost their lives after disembarking from the British ship River Clyde *at V Beach.*

private scampered out of the ship and looked down at a sight he would not soon forget. He explained later that the "water was crystal clear and we could see, lying on the bottom, in perfect formation, the uniformed bodies of the soldiers who had been hit or had fallen while scrambling ashore."[23]

However, since so few Turks defended the beach—less than one hundred fought at W and V Beaches—survivors eventually gained a foothold. The Turks proved with deadly emphasis that they could battle with the best. Great Britain lost twenty thousand soldiers in that first bloody day at the two beaches.

Stalemate at Gallipoli

Over the next few months Hamilton tried to mount attacks to capture the high ground but each time the Turks, led by stalwart men like Kemal, turned them aside. In a June 4 assault, more than thirty thousand British and French forces charged what they thought was the Turkish line, only to find a dummy trench built by the enemy as a trap. Decimating fire swept the Allies from the real trenches beyond.

Human tragedy marked the fighting along the shore. A sniper killed Private Jim Scotson as he stood next to his father, who collapsed in shock and had to be sent home because of a nervous breakdown. Nearby, brothers Fred and Harry Tenant battled together until a bullet killed Harry. Fred later wrote their mother that Harry "fell with his face to the enemy, and I am sure no man could wish for a more glorious death."[24] Within three weeks Fred had also been killed.

In another assault, New Zealand troops faced Mustafa Kemal's men at the ridge of Chunuk Bair. Kemal calmed the men he was about to send into battle by saying, "Don't rush it, my sons. Don't be in a hurry.

We will choose exactly the right minute, then I shall go out in front. When you see me raise my hand, look to it that you have your bayonets sharp and fixed, and come out after me."[25]

The men gazed across at the British lines and waited for Kemal's command. When he lifted his hand and started to

The Flies

Nature frequently affects men in battle. Blinding snowstorms, mud that clutches at soldiers' feet, unspeakable cold, and withering heat are mentioned in many accounts, but one aspect that has often been overlooked is the role played by one of the smallest creatures—flies. In the fighting on the Gallipoli Peninsula, bloated bodies lay for days in the sun and attracted flies by the millions. One British soldier, A. P. Herbert, wrote a poem about a June 4 battle in which he refers to the pests. The poem is included in Martin Gilbert's *The First World War: A Complete History*.

> This is the Fourth of June
>   Think not I never dream
> The noise of that infernal noon,
>   The stretchers' endless stream,
> The tales of triumph won,
>   The night that found them lies,
> The wounded wailing in the sun,
>   The dead, the dust, the flies.
>
> The flies! oh God, the flies
>   That soiled the sacred dead.
> To see them swarm from dead men's eyes
>   And share the soldiers' bread!
> Nor think I now forget
>   The filth and stench of war,
> The corpses on the parapet,
>   The maggots in the floor.

calmly walk toward the British, the other Turks followed and swept to victory.

Since few lulls interrupted the fighting, neither side had an opportunity to retrieve the dead. Millions of flies, attracted by the decaying bodies, swarmed around the battlefields, and a sickening stench enveloped the area. Eventually, both sides agreed to a truce so that men could help the wounded and carry away the dead. Soldiers wearing special white armbands dropped their weapons, stepped out of trenches, and began the gruesome work of removing their fallen comrades. Turks and Brits worked side by side, often exchanging small items or cigarettes and conversing in rough English. Mustafa Kemal supposedly put on a sergeant's uniform and worked for nine hours among the bodies, all the time casting furtive glances toward the English lines to learn what he could about their dispositions. At the end of the day, the enemies shook hands, returned to their own lines, and resumed the killing.

Even though the Allies mounted the Dardanelles operation partly to break the stalemate in western Europe, where trenches dominated the landscape, a similar phenomenon occurred in Gallipoli. After the initial invasion and succeeding attacks, both armies dug trenches and established defensive lines. The same nightmare that gripped France had descended upon Turkey. Winston Churchill's brother, Jack, present at Gallipoli, wrote Winston as early as May 9, "It has become siege warfare again as in France."[26]

An Attempt to Break the Stalemate

British military officials decided in late July that Hamilton needed more troops if he were to break out of the trenches and seize higher land. Hamilton planned advances at Cape Helles and Anzac Cove with three extra divisions, while other men landed at Suvla Bay to the north. These fresh troops planned to move inland, join with the Anzacs from Anzac Cove, and trap the Turkish forces to the south.

This attempt enjoyed no more success than earlier ones. The Turks repulsed the charges at Cape Helles and Anzac Cove, and British incompetence ruined chances of success at Suvla Bay. Although two divisions surprised the Turks at Suvla and landed without opposition, instead of speeding inland the British forces again halted. During the lull, General Sanders rushed reinforcements led by Mustafa Kemal into the region.

Within one day the fighting stalled here as elsewhere. British officers and men exhibited amazing courage, but they failed to dislodge the Turks from the dominating heights. Captain Gerald O'Sullivan rallied his fifty men with the cry, "One more charge for the honor of the regiment,"[27] but only one man survived the pointless advance. The Allies suffered forty thousand casualties in the month of August alone.

The months dragged on in wearying conformity. Attack, kill, and retreat was broken only by miserable stretches in trenches and equally harsh weather. One November storm inundated troops on both sides with twenty-four hours of torrential rains, then followed with sleet and two feet of snow. Water and slush gushed down gullies and ravines, forcing men out of dugouts and drowning or freezing to death at least five hundred soldiers.

Conditions so deteriorated for the Allies that government officials in England lost their jobs. Churchill resigned his post as head of the Admiralty, while General Sir Charles Munro replaced General Hamilton. The cautious Munro made a quick inspection of the Allied lines on Gallipoli, concluded that nothing positive could be achieved, then recommended that all troops be evacuated.

"He came, he saw, he capitulated,"[28] said Winston Churchill of Munro, but there was not much else the British commander could

do. Thousands of men had lost their lives, only to establish on the Gallipoli Peninsula the same set of affairs that existed in France. In eight months of combat the Allies lost 265,000 killed, wounded, or missing, while the Turks suffered 300,000 casualties. New Zealand sent 8,566 men to Gallipoli, yet those soldiers recorded 14,720 casualties, which meant that many were wounded two and three times. Half of all the troops committed to the engagement died or were wounded.

In practically the only successful phase of the Gallipoli fiasco, from December 28 to January 9, 1916, Munro executed the

British troops repeatedly attacked and retreated in Turkey. The only successful action launched by the British was the final evacuation of their forces.

evacuation. Weary men silently filtered out of their dugouts and trenches, meandered down the ridges and ravines, and boarded transports back to Egypt. The Allies so cleverly masked their evacuation—they slowly pulled men down from the front in groups as small as five or six and packed sandbags on paths to muffle the sounds of walking—that the Turks never discovered what had happened until it was over. Not one casualty was taken.

An irate Mustafa Kemal exploded when he learned the enemy had so cleanly slipped away. The courageous Turk, who had done so much to blunt the Allied drive but was not present for this battle, exclaimed to those near him, "Had I been there, and had the British got away without loss, as they did, I would have blown my brains out."[29]

However, Turkey's ally, Germany, admired Munro's skill at extricating his men. One German newspaper gushed, "As long as wars last, the evacuation of Suvla and Anzac will stand before the eyes of all strategists as a hitherto unattained masterpiece."[30] The Germans could afford to be generous when their foe's only successful maneuver was to withdraw from the battlefield. They delivered an appropriate epithet for an ill-advised operation.

Chapter 3

Verdun: The Siege of France's Fortress

With the opposing armies in western Europe mired in trench warfare, military planners on both sides tried to craft battle plans that would turn the momentum in their favor. The British and French devised full-scale assaults against the Germans in the Somme region, while German general Erich von Falkenhayn promoted an intricate plan to remove France from the war and force Great Britain back to home territory. Similar to most operations yet conducted in the war, both strategies failed to achieve their purposes. However, the French would forever remember the valorous conduct of its soldiers in front of one of its most cherished locales—Verdun.

Target Verdun

Falkenhayn, commander of German troops, believed that if the proper target were selected for a new offensive, France would divert all its effort into halting the drive. Falkenhayn argued that if such a situation

arose, his forces could decimate the French Army and leave France so weakened that Britain would be left alone on the western front.

The German general outlined his proposal in a December 1915 letter to Kaiser Wilhelm. He claimed that the "strain on France has reached breaking point. If we succeed in opening the eyes of her people to the fact that in a military sense they have nothing more to hope for, that breaking point would be reached" and England would be on her own. He added that he had to center the offensive on a portion of France so revered that the country would have "to throw in every man they have. If they do so the forces of France will bleed to death."[31]

Falkenhayn chose the French fortress at Verdun as his target. Since the glorious days of the Roman Empire, Verdun held historic significance. Attila the Hun had once attacked the spot, and it was at Verdun in A.D. 843 that the heirs of Emperor Charlemagne divided the remnants of Charlemagne's empire into French and German sections. In the seventeenth century the heralded French military engineer Sébastien Vauban had fortified the town into a formidable bastion able to withstand the most determined sieges. During World War I, this fortification was used to shield Verdun and its nearby city of fourteen thousand citizens by surrounding the main fortress with a series of smaller forts, including Fort Vaux and Fort Douaumont.

To ensure victory, Falkenhayn assembled a frightening display of offensive power. One thousand guns capable of hurling 2.5 million shells at the French backed the 1 million soldiers who stealthily moved into camouflaged forward positions called *stollen*. Poor weather hampered French efforts to spot the buildup in front of Verdun, and as the opening barrage approached, the French defenders remained unaware that the area was about to explode.

Because most of the fighting in the west had occurred far from Verdun, the French in the region had been lulled to inaction. In light of the disastrous opening advance in 1914, when Belgian forts had been quickly neutralized, many of the largest French guns had been removed from the complex of twenty-five forts in the Verdun region. French battalions had been transferred from the lines to serve elsewhere, so that as

German general Erich von Falkenhayn believed the British would be left to fight alone if French forces were eliminated.

the one million German troops moved into position, barely half that number opposed them.

Falkenhayn intended to launch his attack on February 12, 1916, but a miserable mixture of rain, snow, and sleet forced him to postpone the action. German soldiers waited uncomfortably in their unheated, damp *stollen* for nine draining days before

Falkenhayn issued the command to go on the offensive.

The Hellish Barrage

French soldiers rested in their trenches in the quiet predawn moments of February 21, relaxing with a cup of coffee or grabbing a fast meal. Suddenly, the calm erupted in a titanic explosion of sound and fury as the first of 2 million German shells over a twelve-hour bombardment tore into the scenic countryside and smashed against French fortifications. One thousand guns across an eight-mile front hurled 1,667 shells into French lines every minute. In the war's heaviest bombardment to date, mounds of earth tossed up by the shells buried French soldiers alive before they could put down their coffee cups, destroyed communication lines and artillery positions, and uprooted trees. Seven thousand horses perished in a single day. French aviators flying overhead stared in awe at an uninterrupted line of fire belching out from the German positions.

Terrified French soldiers fled their trenches to avoid death, only to meet it in another spot. Hundreds rushed to nearby woods for shelter but were torn apart by falling tree fragments. Out of one group of twelve hundred soldiers, eleven hundred

A German rifleman fights next to the body of a French soldier in what was the war's heaviest bombardment to date.

perished on this ghastly day. A corporal reported that out of every five men in his unit, "two have been buried alive under their shelter, two are wounded to one extent or other, and the fifth is waiting."[32]

Men cracked under the strain of the intense shelling. One French soldier recalled,

When you hear the whistling in the distance your entire body preventively crunches together to prepare for the enormous explosions. Every new explosion is a new attack, a new fatigue, a new affliction. Even nerves of the hardest of steel, are not capable of dealing with this kind of pressure. It is as if you are tied to a pole and threatened by a man with a hammer. First the hammer is swung backwards in order to hit hard, then it is swung forwards, only missing your skull by an inch, into the splintering pole. In the end you just surrender. There is even hardly enough strength left to pray to God.[33]

Falkenhayn's soldiers then rushed from their *stollen* toward the French, whom they expected to be either dead or wounded or completely demoralized from the stunning half-day barrage. German officers turned their hats around so French sharpshooters would not recognize them, then led their men forward. They met sporadic resistance, but most French soldiers could not fire their weapons because dirt from the barrage had filled the barrels and buried their ammunition and grenades. As a result, within three days the German Army advanced three miles deeper into French territory.

French officers begged for help to stop the unceasing German attack. One lieutenant reported that "The commanding officer and all company commanders have been killed. My battalion is reduced to approximately 180 men [from 600]. I have neither ammunition nor food. What am I to do?"[34]

With the French Army in disarray, German soldiers advanced everywhere along the right bank of the Meuse River. On February 24 the French outer line of trenches collapsed, and the next day Fort Douaumont, once considered the anchor of the French defensive line, fell when a solitary German officer worked his way into the fort and captured the remaining fifty-seven French defenders.

Bitter hand-to-hand combat flared in the village of Douaumont on February 28, where French and German soldiers battled with knives, bayonets, and fists as a blinding snowstorm engulfed the region. German units suffered horrendous losses to match those of the French—two thousand of thirty-five hundred men in one sector were killed or wounded. Finally, on March 3, the surviving French forces in the village surrendered, and the French fell back to the final hillside shielding Verdun itself.

The fall of Fort Douaumont and the nearby village ended the battle's first phase, a portion totally dominated by the Germans. Church bells rang in jubilation in

Charles de Gaulle

A man destined to play a prominent role in France's future fought at the battle of Verdun. Captain Charles DeGaulle served as an infantry officer when, during the fighting near Fort Vaux, he was wounded by a bayonet thrust through his thigh and captured on March 2 by the Germans.

The Germans transported the wounded officer to a military hospital in Mainz, then to the first of several prisoner-of-war camps in which he would be confined.

De Gaulle gave his captors no rest, as he attempted to escape on several occasions. One time he made it to within sixty miles of freedom before being recaptured, but the unfortunate Frenchman was doomed to remain in prison camps for the remainder of the war.

Following his release, de Gaulle studied military tactics and politics. When World War II started in 1939, he commanded an armored division as the youngest general in the French Army. While other French forces performed miserably against the triumphant Germans, de Gaulle's unit fought splendidly.

When most of France surrendered to the Germans in June 1940, de Gaulle fled to England to rally supporters. For the rest of the war he symbolized resistance to Nazi tyranny as leader of the Free French forces. After the war ended, de Gaulle served as French president and helped rebuild the nation. He died in 1970.

Charles de Gaulle made several escape attempts while he was a prisoner of war and became the president of France after World War II.

Germany and schoolchildren received a special holiday to mark the occasion. Newspapers in Berlin and other major cities boasted that the French were on the verge of collapse. However, the Germans did not count on the astounding resilience and willpower of their foes who, with their backs to the wall and facing dire threats to Verdun and France itself, stepped forward to halt the offensive.

"We Shall Bear Up"

Two soldiers typified French defiance. When the German ruler Kaiser Wilhelm visited the front, he asked to meet Lieutenant Colonel Bernard, a French officer who had been captured in the battle's opening moments. Instead of a broken individual, the Kaiser encountered a determination that would become a trademark for the remainder of the battle. Bernard, captured but not beaten, warned the German ruler, "You will never enter Verdun."[35]

The other individual stepped into the maelstrom, reorganized the confused French forces, and vowed that the Germans would be rebuffed. Led by a man who would become a national hero, sixty-year-old General Philippe Pétain, the French turned disaster into glory.

Pétain had been in command on February 25 barely one hour before he informed his officers that the Germans had taken the last piece of French soil. He ordered them to retake any territory already lost to the enemy, and announced to one of his top generals, "I am taking over. Inform your troops. Keep up your courage." Heartened by Pétain's optimism, the general replied, "Very well, sir, we shall bear up. You can rely on us, as we rely on you."[36]

Pétain, later honored as the hero of Verdun, realized that to stem the German advance, supplies and reinforcements had to

Faced with a military and national disaster, General Philippe Pétain kept the French fighting by organizing a massive relief effort to get supplies and troops to the city of Verdun.

be rushed to the front. He declared the solitary road leading into Verdun as a supply route, banned other traffic, and organized an around-the-clock flow of supplies. Soldiers marching forward had to exit the road and use adjoining fields to make room for the torrent of trucks that breathed life into Verdun on a twenty-four hour basis. Pétain stationed thousands of soldiers along the road to quickly repair damaged portions and to throw dirt into holes; they shoved to the side any vehicles that broke down to allow the following trucks to pass. Pétain so efficiently organized the relief effort that two supply trucks arrived in Verdun every minute. In all, 190,000 reinforcements and 23,000 tons of supplies kept France's soldiers fighting at Verdun.

At the Battle of Verdun, French troops react as they come under fire from a German artillery barrage.

The Crucial Battle of the Hills

Falkenhayn faced another problem besides Pétain's determination. Falkenhayn had been concentrating his attacks on the right bank of the Meuse River while allowing the left bank to remain in French hands. As a result, French artillery inflicted heavy casualties whenever the Germans tried to move forward. Falkenhayn decided to launch a new offensive on the left bank to eliminate this threat, especially that posed by French defenders implanted on two hills—Le Mort Homme and Hill 304.

The drive, which opened on March 6, 1916, kicked off two months of combat in the most miserable conditions at Le Mort Homme. A seemingly endless cycle gripped the fighting: German attack would achieve minor gains before slowing, then the inevitable French counterattack would push them back to their original lines. Each time, fresh bodies lying atop the contested ground served as gruesome evidence of the repetitive slaughter. Artillery shells churned the dirt again and again, tossing decaying remains into charred trees and demolishing whatever semblance of trenches remained. Snow, torrential rain, and sleet transformed the region into a muddy morass that sucked the boots off soldiers' feet, halted movement, and immobilized the combatants. Wounded French and German soldiers, unable to crawl from shell holes, drowned as rainwater cascaded into their shelters.

Sometimes, one man made a difference. A French officer named Macker calmly directed his troops in a successful counterattack. Ignoring the German machine gun bullets that ripped into the ground inches from his feet, Macker, puffing a cigar and brandishing a cane, walked directly toward the German positions. Emboldened by this display of bravery, his men swarmed toward the enemy lines and forced the Germans in that area to retreat. Later in the day Macker and a fellow officer were chatting when machine gun fire killed both. Demoralized by the absence of their leader, the French fell back in the face of a strong German counterattack.

The daily horrors of combat ground down even the sturdiest of men, causing an increase of insubordination and defection on both sides. Men refused to leave their shelters, and groups of soldiers surrendered rather than endure further misery. One German officer said "the front soldiers become numb by seeing the bodies without heads, without legs, shot through the belly, with blown away foreheads, with holes in their chests."[37]

On the other side of the lines a French soldier battled a sense of doom. "Soon the losses became more and more. Every soldier is simply waiting in quiet acceptance for the grenade that has his name on it. And everywhere there is screaming and moaning, sirens and crackle, dirt and blood, death and dying."[38] To keep his soldiers at the front lines and slow the rate of desertion, one French officer moved a machine gun near him in case he had to turn it on his own men.

The Germans launched a second major effort on April 9, but it, too, failed to achieve anything beyond additional death and destruction. Artillery shells blasted Hill 304 with such thoroughness that it removed six feet of dirt from its height, and officers recorded instances of men going mad under the strain. Pétain later wrote:

> My heart leapt as I saw our youths of twenty going into the furnace of Verdun. But how depressing it was when they returned. Their expressions seemed frozen by a vision of terror; their gait and their postures betrayed a total dejection; they sagged beneath the weight of horrifying memories.[39]

For two months the Germans mounted unsuccessful attempts to seize both hills from the French. Finally, near the end of May, the Germans stormed the summits and gained a glimpse down toward Verdun itself. Across the Meuse, other German units advanced on Fort Vaux and, after a fierce fight with French defenders, seized the fort.

The Germans acquired their objectives, but at a high price to both sides. Two months of combat cost the Germans eighty-two thousand deaths, while eighty-nine thousand Frenchmen perished defending Verdun. These locations represented the farthest advance made by Falkenhayn's forces. For the next six months the antagonists stood their ground and battled like two exhausted boxers trying to stay on their feet.

The Fatal Gamble

A change in command brought a change in French tactics. General Robert Nivelle succeeded Pétain, who had been ordered to a different sector to halt a new German drive. Nivelle, an artillery specialist, organized the most deadly concentration of artillery fire Verdun had seen. During May and June, 20 million shells disrupted German concentrations, demolished German positions, and stripped the land of most foliage. When Falkenhayn's forces still advanced closer to Verdun, Nivelle rallied both French soldier and citizen alike with the stirring order, "They shall not pass!"[40]

Again the opposing military entered a brutal slugfest that sapped life and drained hope. One French soldier, weary of the endless carnage, moaned, "Having despaired of living amid such horror, we begged God to let us be dead."[41] A German infantryman wrote that bodies bloated and decayed faster in the summer heat, requiring the survivors to stuff garlic in their nostrils to reduce the stench.

The Germans launched a final offensive against Verdun on July 11 in hopes of cracking through the French defenses. After bitter fighting, the French halted the drive, and although fighting still flared, both sides settled into a three-month lull.

The French carefully marshaled their forces to organize an October attack against the German lines. By early November they had shoved the Germans out of the fallen French forts, and before year's end the French had regained much of the ground lost in the spring. The Germans, who could

A Hero to Both Sides

One officer who earned accolades from both his own French forces and from the Germans he opposed was Lieutenant Colonel Emile Driant. According to Alistair Horne's account, *The Price of Glory: Verdun 1916,* as the battle raged and men started fleeing from the swarm of German attackers, Driant calmly stepped out of his command post with a rifle in hand and rallied his men by saying, "We are here. This is our place. They shall not move us out of it."

Bullets kicked up ground on all sides of the courageous Driant, causing some of his men to beg him to seek cover. "You know very well they've

never hit me yet!" he responded. In spite of his efforts, the Germans forced Driant's men backward. As the French retreated through an open field, Driant halted to help a wounded comrade. Before he could offer much assistance, he threw his hands into the air, screamed, "Oh, my God!" and slumped dead to the ground.

The Germans had been impressed with the gallantry displayed by Driant. His personal effects were later retrieved by a German officer, who sent them home to his wife in Germany. She forwarded them to Driant's widow in a fitting tribute to bravery from one opponent to another.

Reinforced by supplies and troops rushed in by General Pétain, the French managed to withstand the German onslaught and save Verdun.

not commit the needed men or material because so much had been diverted to battle the British drive in the Somme region, realized their action near Verdun had failed.

Falkenhayn's gamble to capture venerable Verdun, sap French strength, and demoralize the enemy had instead produced catastrophic results for the Germans. Had Falkenhayn succeeded in capturing Verdun in the spring, he might have so demoralized the French that they might have asked for peace. This could have enabled the Germans to then rush their forces eastward to knock out the Russians, which would have left Great Britain standing alone. The course of the war could have been altered at Verdun in Germany's favor. Instead, momentum swung in favor of the French. Before the fighting at Verdun, Germany had a chance to win the war; afterward, it never again posed as significant a threat. As a result, Kaiser Wilhelm replaced Falkenhayn as commander.

A Frightful New Weapon

The Germans introduced a new weapon during their assault at Verdun. On February 21 German foot soldiers stepped onto the battlefield bearing strange devices on their backs and clutching what looked like metallic hoses in their hands. To the horror of French defenders, the Germans pointed the hoses toward French defenders and blanketed them with a lethal stream of fire. The flamethrower had made its ignoble debut.

With uniforms afire and men screaming for help, burning Frenchmen rushed out of their positions to either crumble to a blazing death or to be mercifully shot by advancing Germans. For a time, whenever the French spotted a flamethrower they fled the area. Within a few days, however, French sharpshooters learned to target the Germans bearing the new device. They did not even have to hit the man to be effective—a single bullet into the flamethrower produced a fiery explosion that engulfed both the German handling the flamethrower and any soldiers unfortunate enough to be near him. Though soldiers on the battlefield still feared the hideous weapon, they at least had some defense against it.

Intended as a weapon of terror, the Germans unleashed the flamethrower during the Verdun campaign.

The eight-month battle in front of Verdun ended with opposing sides back where they started and no end in sight to the interminable slaughter. In saving the nation's honor, France lost 542,000 men killed, wounded, missing, or as prisoners of war near Verdun, while Falkenhayn's plan cost the Germans 434,000 soldiers. In a war already notorious for its appalling death tolls, Verdun held the dubious distinction of producing the highest density of dead soldiers per square yard of any World War I battle.

In sad testament, a memorial plaque currently rests at Fort Vaux, mounted by a French mother and dedicated to her fallen son. The plaque bears the simple but powerful inscription: TO MY SON, SINCE YOUR EYES WERE CLOSED MINE HAVE NEVER CEASED TO CRY. [42]

Berlin newspapers could no longer boast of victory, and German church bells failed to resonate with triumph. Since enemy forces still occupied much of their territory, the French could not be too boastful; they had merely shoved back an attack, not defeated a foe. More fighting and dying awaited before the war would be determined.

What high-ranking officers might not comprehend, the common foot soldier did. Exasperated with the lack of progress, in spite of the killing and maiming, German and French soldiers gazed into a future that held little promise other than death or injury. One German soldier, on the verge of despair, wrote his family that the fighting would continue "until the last German and the last Frenchman hobbled out of the trenches on crutches to exterminate each other with pocket knives or teeth and finger nails." [43] The unheralded German accurately predicted the war's path as it wound its way out of 1916 and into 1917.

Chapter 4

The Somme: The Slaughter of Britain's Youth

S till weary from the combat around Verdun, the French begged Great Britain to open an offensive else-where along the western front that would divert German troops from Verdun and ease the pressure on the beleaguered French. The British agreed to launch an attack at the Somme—a river halfway between Paris and the North Sea coast—and named General Sir Douglas Haig to head the operation.

The plan, as always, called for a massive preassault artillery barrage. Even though these had failed to demolish defenses in previous battles, Allied generals continued to believe in their effectiveness, and so once again, soldiers marched into battle expecting little or no opposition from dazed German defenders, but instead received a murderous welcome.

Faith in the Artillery

Haig called for a week-long bombardment, after which a combined British-French force would strike on a twenty-mile front along both sides of the Somme. The attacks to the right and left flanks provided diversion for the main effort in the middle, by British general Sir Henry Rawlinson's 4th Army. The main effort was to punch through enemy lines between the towns of Maricourt and Fricourt, advance several miles, then hold off the Germans as a cavalry charge broke into the German rear, disrupted lines of communications and unit headquarters, and swept into Cambrai twenty-five miles beyond.

Haig placed so much faith in the artillery barrage that he issued an order that doomed twenty thousand men. Instead of allowing the soldiers to cross No-Man's-Land (an unoccupied area between opposing armies) in a maneuver called "fire and movement," in which some soldiers lay down and provide a covering fire as the other soldiers advance, Haig ordered each unit to march in straight lines, tightly together, for the entire five thousand yards to the German lines. His confidence in a barrage that had proven useless elsewhere led to more disaster at the Somme.

Instead of seasoned troops, Haig sent into battle recent arrivals from England, where only months before they had volunteered with schoolmates and neighborhood friends. They entered together, trained together, and at the Somme they died together, costing England many of her finest young men. Thirteen battalions came from the towns of Yorkshire and Lancashire alone. The 16th Middlesex gained the nickname "the Public School Battalion," and the 10th Lincolns called themselves "the Grimsby Chums."

Haig should have realized that he was sending soldiers into a maelstrom, not just at the Somme, but everywhere along the western front the Germans had constructed almost indestructible defenses. They drove

After emerging from their trench, British troops were given orders to march together in straight lines, a move that resulted in catastrophe.

dugouts at the Somme thirty feet into the ground so they could withstand even the harshest artillery barrage. Underground communications cables linked each forward position to command posts in the rear, machine guns protected every avenue of approach across No-Man's-Land, and miles of barbed wire stood in front of the trenches. Eight months of effort allowed the Germans to map each yard of No-Man's-Land and assign guns to cover the sections.

The French terrain assisted the Germans. The Allies would have to cross three miles of open land, then attack along a gradual slope, meaning the Germans would be shooting down from concealed positions while the Allies had to climb up. Conditions were in place for a charge that one historian labeled "the single worst day in the entire military history of their [English] country."[44]

Haig's bombardment commenced on June 24 when fifteen hundred guns—one for every twenty yards of German-occupied land—opened fire along the twenty-mile front. The guns were supposed to demolish the strings of barbed wire, collapse German dugouts, and crush trenches. Then, to keep surviving German defenders from leaving their shelters and manning their posts too quickly, a rolling barrage would precede the Allied troops as they advanced across No-Man's-Land.

As in other attacks, the bombardment failed to achieve any of its purposes. Many of Haig's shells failed to detonate, and the ones that did were not powerful enough to destroy the sturdy dugouts. Instead of removing the barbed wire, the explosions simply tossed the wire into the air, then dropped it back onto the ground more gnarled and jangled than before. A British raid into the German trenches that was scheduled a few days before the main assault learned that, despite the heavy shelling, the dugouts appeared relatively unharmed.

"They Are Coming"

The British and French left their trenches on July 1, spurred by discipline, youthful eagerness, and false hopes. Before many had

Douglas Haig

The British commander at the Somme, Douglas Haig, was not a typical officer. A devout Christian who felt he had a direct line of communication with God, Haig also believed in the powers of séances. Once in his early career a medium supposedly put Haig in contact with the spirit of Napoleon, the famous French ruler and military leader from the 1800s. Quiet and reserved, Haig showed no emotion over the slaughters that marked the western front, contending that this was a cross that he, and in more drastic form, the soldiers, had to bear.

Douglas Haig was a British commander who believed he could directly communicate with God.

advanced twenty yards, German machine gun fire tore into their ranks. Men stumbled in depressions in the ground or momentarily stepped back in fright, tossing the advancement off schedule.

The rolling barrage, which ideally would precede the soldiers fifty yards ahead and gradually churn toward the German lines, also failed to work properly. Since the infantry had no means of communicating with the artillerymen, it was impossible to coordinate the barrage. Artillerymen simply fired shells at a set location for a set time, then automatically moved forward fifty yards.

On the open ground, however, British infantry could not keep to a precise timetable. Burdened with 66 pounds of equipment, including sandbags, 220 rounds of ammunition, a rifle, a shovel, and other items, they lurched forward, fell back a few yards, tried to ignore bullets that smacked around them, and slowly moved toward the opposing lines. One of the more frightening moments occurred when the front line of British soldiers watched their own artillery barrage move beyond the German trenches without touching the defenders, who quickly manned their machine guns and began a slaughter.

The Germans waited until the bombardment passed by, then rushed to their posts. One German soldier, F. L. Cassell, recalled

> the shout of the sentry, "They are coming." Helmet, belt and rifle and up the steps. In the trench a headless body. The

sentry had lost his life to a last shell. There they come, the [British]. They are not twenty meters in front of our trench. They advance slowly fully - equipped. Machine-gun fire tears holes in their ranks."[45]

Even for the western front, which had seen a full measure of death, the slaughter at the Somme on July 1 set new standards of hideousness. British soldiers fell with wounds, only to be hit in succession by two or three more bullets. The 1st Newfoundland Regiment of 750 men disintegrated before it reached the German lines. When the firing died down, all 26 officers and 658 men lay dead or wounded.

One British sergeant moved with his men as they advanced across No-Man's-Land, maintaining a near-perfect line in the chaos. Every yard brought more death, though. He later revealed,

> Away to my left and right, long lines of men. Then I heard the "patter, patter" of machine guns in the distance. By the time I'd gone another ten yards there seemed to be only a few men left around me; by the time I had gone twenty yards, I seemed to be on my own. Then I was hit myself.[46]

The agonies suffered by the British contrasted with the relative safety for the Germans is illustrated by the German 180th Regiment. Its 3,000 men suffered 180 casualties, while the 12,000 British soldiers who

marched toward its lines lost 5,121 men. The slaughter eventually became so sickening that many German machine gunners stopped firing their weapons so that British wounded could return to their lines.

Of the hundred thousand British soldiers who left the trenches that morning, twenty thousand died and another forty thousand lay wounded by day's end. Thirty-two different battalions suffered casualties of more than 60 percent, and a few, like the 1st Newfoundland, ceased to exist. The losses exceeded the combined casualties suffered by Great Britain in three of its wars—the Crimean War, Boer War, and Korean War.

Even still, the brutal message failed to impress Allied generals, who continued to insist that the tactics that had repeatedly

The magnitude of the the carnage visited upon British soldiers at the Somme stunned even their German opponents.

failed would one day end the war. Rather than disgust and shock, pride registered on their faces.

The reaction of Brigadier General H. C. Rees, the commander of the 94th Infantry Brigade, was typical. He reported to superiors that his men "advanced in line after line, dressed as if on parade, and not a man shirked going through the extremely heavy barrage, or facing the machine gun and rifle fire that finally wiped them out. [It was] a magnificent display of gallantry, discipline and determination."[47]

No Gains, Many Losses

The fighting at the Somme now dissolved into a stalemate to equal that found in front of Verdun. A series of raids mounted by both sides did little but add to the toll of misery and death. Men wounded in No-Man's-Land often died before they reached safe lines. Others lay in the open for a week before being brought in.

On July 14 Haig hurled a second attack against the Germans, but this faltered as quickly as the first. By the end of July the Allies had suffered 200,000 casualties with little movement in the front lines. Since the Germans had begun staging their own raids to retrieve any lost territory, their losses mounted appallingly during this time as well—160,000 men were lost in one month.

To add to their woes, heavy rains turned the fighting area into an arena of mud. Soldiers ordered to attack quickly slowed their pace because of the mud that clutched at their feet and gathered about their boots. Caught in the open by enemy machine guns and unable to hastily retreat because of the mud, men made perfect targets for gunners.

British captain D. C. Stephenson wrote to his mother of a raid in which he had participated:

I had a nasty experience yesterday. Another gunner officer and I, with one of my signallers, were reconnoitering a very new trench the Germans have dug. We got a good long way out in No Man's

Some of the wounded lay out in the open for a week before they were brought back to the relative safety of the rear lines.

Land and suddenly got severely sniped at. The other officer got back safely, and my signaller and I started to crawl back. All of a sudden he got up for some reason and ran. He hadn't gone two steps before he spun round and fell, just in front of me. I plugged up his wound as well as I could, and then a very gallant infantryman came out, on his own, to help me dress him. This man raised his head for a moment while bandaging, and then fell, shot through the head and helmet, on top of me.[48]

Robert Graves, a noted English poet, sneaked out of his own trenches one night to search for a heavier coat. As he hugged the ground he came across a sight he would never forget—a British and a German soldier who had simultaneously bayoneted each other, leaning in death in an upright position against a tree trunk.

As the fighting ebbed and flowed, certain positions had to be momentarily yielded to the enemy, then retaken a few days later. The dead often remained unburied in the trenches until their comrades returned, who then frequently filled in the trench with dirt to provide a hasty cemetery. When British forces reoccupied a position once defended by men from Devonshire, they found the bodies of British soldiers scattered about one trench. After covering the slain men and the trench with dirt, the men posted a sign: THE DEVONSHIRES HELD THIS TRENCH: THE DEVONSHIRES HOLD IT STILL. [49]

Siegfried Sassoon

British soldier Siegfried Sassoon gained fame as a poet before serving in the war. During his time in European battlefields, Sassoon observed some of the harshest combat and later compiled his experiences into a classic book, *Memoirs of an Infantry Officer*. The following quote, taken from that volume, describes the effect war has upon humans who would normally be considered civilized.

> As the day went on, I definitely wanted to kill someone at close quarters. If this meant that I was really becoming a good "fighting man," I can only suggest that, as a human being, I was both exhausted and exasperated. My courage was of the cock-fighting kind. Cock-fighting is illegal in England, but in July 1916 the man who could boast that he'd killed a German in the Battle of the Somme would have been patted on the back by a bishop in a hospital ward.

"A Pretty Mechanical Toy"

Haig scheduled another large offensive for September 15. Though its final outcome resembled every other Allied attack over the last year—mounting death tolls in a futile charge—the fighting introduced a new weapon to warfare, one that, if employed properly, might have ended the terrors on the western front. The revolutionary vehicle was the tank.

The idea came from the inventive mind of a British military thinker, Colonel Ernest Swinton. The tank was given its name because the earliest devices reminded onlookers of moveable water tanks. Swinton added armor plating and machine guns to heavy tractors equipped with caterpillar treads. He figured that, since enemy machine gun bullets would deflect off the metallic surface, such a vehicle would be able to cross No-Man's-Land without harm, smash over the barbed wire that had been so effective in halting foot soldiers, lumber across narrow trenches, and churn into the German rear areas.

Swinton's final product carried eight soldiers, droved half a mile for every gallon of gasoline, and advanced at the agonizingly slow rate of 3.7 miles per hour. However, Swinton argued that the tank's speed mattered little because of the heavy plating it carried as protection.

Many top British officials scorned Swinton's invention. Lord Kitchener, the secretary of war and one of the nation's most esteemed military heroes, dismissed the tank as "a pretty mechanical toy but of very limited value."[50] However, the novel idea received the support of one influential man who, when seized by an idea, refused to let go—Winston Churchill. With Churchill's backing, Swinton's invention made it to the front.

Haig decided to put the weapon to the test in his September 15 assault. Thirty-six tanks accompanied the thousands of soldiers who left the trenches, and their initial appearance produced a stunning reaction from the Germans. Terrified of the new apparatus, which spit out its own bullets while ignoring those of the Germans, some German soldiers fled their posts and yielded up to thirty-five hundred yards of territory.

Disaster then struck. Haig rushed the tanks into use before Swinton and Churchill felt it was proper. The tank crews had not been fully trained, and a proper course of strategy for their use had yet to be devised.

Haig's eagerness to witness the tank's usefulness overcame these objections, however.

Haig also erred when he spread out the tanks along a wide area instead of concentrating them in a single, powerful thrust. Acting in unison, the tanks could have brought their overwhelming firepower and numbers against an isolated spot, crashed through to rear areas, and then held on until help arrived from the infantry. Instead, Haig committed the tanks piecemeal, which dissipated their effectiveness. Some tanks lumbered into large shell holes and either took a long time getting out or were never extricated. Others suffered mechanical breakdowns or fell victim to enemy artillery shells. One by one, all thirty-six halted, enabling the

The tank was dismissed by some as an ineffective tool and touted by others to be a powerful weapon.

Germans to reoccupy the positions earlier abandoned.

The tank may have made a dubious debut but it showed that, once perfected, the weapon could be the instrument to alter the conduct of warfare. Unfortunately, most top Allied officers failed to see beyond the incomplete first appearance at the Somme and dismissed the tank's use in the future. In another world war twenty years later, men like General Erwin Rommel of Germany and George Patton of the United States would illustrate the tank's potency with decisive results.

Not every German soldier feared the new Allied device. One corporal who battled from the Somme trenches later wrote, "I was carried away by the enthusiasm and I sank down upon my knees and thanked Heaven out of the fullness of my heart for the honor of having been permitted to live in such a time."[51] The corporal—Adolf Hitler—who was wounded by a shell frag-

Inexperienced tank crews and poor command decisions led to a less than impressive debut for British tanks.

ment on October 7, later went on to gain infamy as Germany's leader during the next world war. Winston Churchill, a definitive voice who favored placing the tanks on the Somme battlefield, would also rise: He served as the British prime minister during World War II. There, he would battle to prevent Europe from being overrun by the youthful corporal—Hitler—sitting in the German trenches along the Somme.

Results

Sporadic fighting followed Haig's September 15 failure. The Germans staged a counteroffensive on September 25, which the British rebuffed, and then the two sides played a game of cat and mouse, with smaller raids being mounted against enemy positions. By mid-November, with autumn

No-Man's-Land

One of the better descriptions of No-Man's-Land comes from soldier and military historian Ernest Swinton, whose inventive mind fashioned the earliest tanks. He participated in some of the thickest fighting of World War I and later wrote an account of what he saw. The material is included in an article by Malcolm Brown which appeared in the summer 1996 issue of *MHQ: The Quarterly Journal of Military History.*

> Seamed with dug-outs, burrows, trenches, and excavations of every kind, and fitted with craters, it is bounded on the front by a long discontinuous irregular line fringed with barbed wire. Beyond, if width varying according to the nature of the fighting and of the ground, is neutral territory, the no-man's-land between the hostile forces. It is strewn with the dead of both sides, some lying, others caught and propped in the sagging wire, where they may have been for days, still others half buried in craters or destroyed parapets. On the other side of this zone of the unburied dead bristles a similar fringe of wire and a long succession of low mounds and parapets—the position of the enemy. And woe betide the man who in daylight puts up his head carelessly to take a long glance at it.

rains transforming the fields into a muddy quagmire that retarded operations, Haig called off the Somme offensive.

The same tragic results appeared at the Somme—battalions of youth tossed away for little or no gains. In another example of the next generation paying for the errors of the preceding one, 420,000 British soldiers died or were wounded at the Somme. France lost 195,000, and Germany amassed 650,000 casualties. In most locations along the front, the lines advanced not even a single yard.

The slaughter proved to be the worst in British history. Winston Churchill stated that the nation lost the cream of its youth and the source of its future leadership, and to a large degree he proved correct.

Nature also felt the effects. The Somme region had been known for its beauty and fertile farmland. Before the battle, trees and flowers mingled with bounteous crops, but a wasteland appeared afterward. One survivor later recalled staring from his trench: "All you could see was a long line of stumps going straight on to nowhere."[52]

Nothing had yet occurred to shake the European combatants from the appalling slaughter along the western front. A new participant appeared, however, which brought hope to the Allied side. The United States, having never before intervened in a European land war, entered on the side of the Allies. Along with their new troops came the hope that the United States could bring a new approach to warfare.

Chapter 5

Belleau Wood

American soldiers arrived in Europe in late 1917, simultaneously bolstering Allied hopes of victory while causing apprehension for the Germans. The addition of thousands of fresh troops would aid the French and British, but no one on either side knew if these green troops could fight. The United States had never battled on European soil, and its most recent engagements had been against the outclassed Spanish Army stationed in Cuba, where the United States enjoyed an easy victory, and on frontier posts, where they swiftly eliminated Native American tribes through forced removal or massacre. Could American infantry and marine units face the Germans, generally considered as the most elite army in the world? Americans, organized in the American Expeditionary Forces (AEF), provided the answer in a forested section of France called Belleau Wood.

A New Confidence

General John J. Pershing, the commander of the AEF, earmarked the 2nd Division for the assault against German forces huddling in Belleau Wood. Consisting of 1,063 officers and 25,602 men spread out among the 23rd U.S. Infantry and the 4th Marine Brigade, the 2nd Division received orders to secure Belleau Wood and the adjoining village of Bouresches so that Germany could no longer use this area as a staging ground for attacks against the Allies. Pershing's chief of staff, Brigadier General James Harbord, assumed command and promised Pershing spectacular results.

Belleau Wood encompassed a smaller area compared to earlier battlegrounds. With only one square mile, the woods contained thousands of trees, most not more than six inches thick, planted so closely together that a traveler could barely see twenty feet ahead. Bushes and dead branches impeded movement and offered choice locations for German machine guns. The Americans had been handed a difficult location for their baptism by fire.

When Harbord and his aides assembled on June 5 to first discuss plans for the attack, a dubious French officer suggested that the inexperienced Americans might consider falling back rather than challenging the mighty German Army. Colonel Wendell C. Neville, commander of the 5th Marine Regiment, rebuffed the insult with words that illustrated the fiery determination that accompanied the uninitiated Americans. The officer quickly replied, "Retreat, hell. We just got here."[53]

Harbord finalized the plans less than twenty-four hours before the advance was to

After years of unrelenting warfare, British and French forces welcomed the arrival of American troops.

begin. Supported by a French regiment to the left and the 23rd Infantry on the right, the marines would rush through fields rich with wheat ready to be harvested and dotted with millions of red poppy flowers, then head into Belleau Wood to do battle with the enemy. The plan, drawn hastily to put American units into battle as quickly as possible, suffered from a lack of general knowledge about the terrain and from an inability to move large guns close to the front for support. Consequently, on June 6 marines and their supporting soldiers would have to file through unscouted fields with little more than their rifles, bayonets, and courage to protect them.

Pershing accepted the risks because he intended to show his European Allies, especially the French, that Americans could fight

as well as any army. One offensive remark on June 1 by a French officer still rankled the American leader, who later explained how he dealt with the abrasive individual.

I intimated that we had had quite enough of this sort of thing from the French, either military or civilian, and suggested that if his people would cease troubling themselves so much about

John Joseph Pershing

John Joseph Pershing, the American army commander, already boasted a distinguished record before World War I. Born in 1860, he was elected president of his class at West Point. Following grad-

uation he served on the American frontier, where he commanded black soldiers in campaigns against the Apache and Sioux Indians, and in the Philippines, where he fought Filipino rebels following the Spanish-American War of 1898.

Shortly before the outbreak of World War I, Pershing, nicknamed "Black Jack" because he had supervised black soldiers, headed an expedition into Mexico to pursue the notorious group of bandits led by Pancho Villa. Tragedy struck when he learned that his wife and three daughters perished in the 1916 San Francisco fire.

One year later he received command of the American Expeditionary Force and led the first American soldiers into the European conflict. In addition to the Germans, he battled French and British generals who hoped to keep the American forces under their supervision.

Pershing returned to the United States after the war to a hero's welcome. Congress handed him the title General of the Armies, an honor previously granted only to George Washington. He retired in 1924 and died in 1948.

General "Black Jack" Pershing, already a battle-hardened soldier, led the first American military forces into the European conflict.

our affairs and attend more strictly to their own we should all get along much better.[54]

Most French citizens did not share the pompous attitude shown by the man who addressed Pershing and eagerly greeted the jubilant Americans. During the night of June 5–6, a thousand trucks packed with American soldiers headed toward the jump-off zones. The long line meandered through tiny French villages bulging with French citizens who cheered the new arrivals and hoped that they would be the remedy to end this lengthy war.

One look at the young men inside the trucks restored faith, for they bore themselves with a different attitude than that carried by French and British infantry who had endured the worst of trench warfare. Bedecked in fresh uniforms, the cocky Yanks joked and laughed as the trucks took them nearer to battle. One French citizen who greeted the Americans said,

Striking was the contrast in appearance between the Americans and the French regiments whose men, in torn uniforms, hungry and hollow-eyed, were scarcely able to hold themselves erect. New life had come to bring a fresh, surging vigor to the body of France, bled almost to death. Thus it came to pass that in those crucial days when the enemy stood for a second time on the Marne [River], thinking us disheartened, then, contrary to all expectation, an ineffable

confidence filled the hearts of all Frenchmen.[55]

A Field of Red Poppies

As a preliminary to the main thrust, at dawn of June 6, 1918, one battalion of the 5th Marine Regiment attacked Hill 142 to the west of Belleau Wood. German fire forced Americans to the ground, where they crawled toward the trees amidst a hail of bullets that killed hundreds of marines in the wheat fields. Stalwart individuals kept the men moving. Captain George Hamilton ran back and forth along the line of marines, telling his men that the only way to avoid death was to charge directly toward their German opponent and kill him before he killed them. With bayonets fixed, the men again rose from the ground, rushed the enemy lines, and grappled with their foe in horrific hand-to-hand combat. Hamilton's five junior officers died in the attack, but here and there a few marines reached the top and began eliminating German machine gun positions.

Hamilton later stated that

I have vague recollections of urging the whole line on, faster, perhaps, than they should have gone—of grouping prisoners and sending them to the rear under one man instead of several—of snatching an iron cross ribbon [German military award] off the first officer I got—and of shooting wildly at several rapidly retreating Boches [slang for Germans].[56]

Hamilton so effectively goaded his men that many raced beyond a ridge that was to be their initial objective and had to be called back out of fear of being hit by their own artillery. Soldiers who had braved enemy fire heading toward the Germans now endured more while moving away from them.

By noon the marines controlled the hill, then engaged in a day-long battle against stiff German counterattacks to keep what they had taken. For brief periods the Germans dislodged the Americans from the crest, only to yield to another determined push by the marines. When darkness settled over the battlefield on June 6, Hill 142 contained a line of weary Americans along its summit.

The major assault jumped off in the afternoon when three battalions of marines hit enemy lines from the west and southwest to take Belleau Wood and Bouresches to the southeast. The men entered the wheat field in neat rows after one of the battalion's commanders, Colonel Albertus Catlin, shouted, "Give 'm hell, boys!"[57]

The inexperienced marines steadily inched toward the woods in a line that wavered under intense German machine gun and rifle fire. Men screamed in pain and dropped to the dirt, while bullets sliced the top halves off the wheat stalks. Thousands of glorious red poppies swayed in the breeze,

Rallied by Gunnery Sergeant Dan Daly, inexperienced American marines advanced into Belleau Wood, engaging in hand-to-hand combat with their German adversaries.

their color being matched by the blood that stained hundreds of marine uniforms.

The slow advance halted until a legendary veteran rallied the frightened men. Gunnery Sergeant Dan Daly had won the nation's highest military award, the Medal of Honor, twenty years earlier in China, then spent the intervening years terrifying fresh marine recruits as a drill instructor with his commanding voice and brusque presence. With more than one hundred yards still to go before reaching the front edge of Belleau Wood, the fearless Daly noticed the faltering green line. Suddenly, the familiar voice boomed above the din of battle, "Come on, you sons of bitches! Do you want to live forever?"[58] Emboldened marines, led by the indomitable Daly, renewed the charge.

Casualties mounted. Sergeant Merwin Silverthorn accompanied his lieutenant in an advance up a ravine. When Silverthorn and the officer reached the top, the lieutenant looked back to see nothing but open fields. "Where the hell is my platoon?"[59] he shouted to Silverthorn. Of the fifty-two men with which he began the attack, forty-six had been shot.

The two battalions of the 6th Marine Regiment enjoyed better fortune to the east, where they had to cross a shorter stretch of open ground before reaching Belleau Wood. Accompanying them was *Chicago Tribune* correspondent Floyd Gibbons, who arrived near the front lines moments before the 6th Regiment was to move out. When an officer asked him why he came to such a dangerous spot, Gibbons responded he was looking for a newsworthy story. The marine officer examined the reporter as if he were crazy, then said, "If I were you I'd be about forty miles south of this place, but if you want to see the fun stick around. We are going forward in about five minutes."[60]

Along with the marines, Gibbons hit the ground when the firing became too intense. At one point in the battle he crawled over to help a wounded marine, but stopped when he felt a pain burn his left arm as if he had just been singed by a lit cigarette. When he examined the wound, he discovered that a bullet had gone completely through. A second bullet nicked his left shoulder, then a third shattered his left eye and forehead. When a nearby marine asked Gibbons to raise his head so he could check the dam-

Wartime Classic

War produces a torrent of literature, ranging from poems to histories to fiction. One of the most highly regarded works on World War I came from the pen of the German author, Erich Maria Remarque, who wrote the memorable *All Quiet on the Western Front*. Seen from the viewpoint of German soldiers, the book presents a searing image of war's destruction. At one point in the story, Remarque comments on the fighting on the western front that aged the young men and destroyed their hopes.

> We are not youth any longer. We don't want to take the world by storm. We are fleeing. We fly from ourselves. From our life. We were eighteen and had begun to love life and the world; and we had to shoot it to pieces. The first bomb, the first explosion, burst in our hearts. We are cut off from activity, from striving, from progress. We believe in such things no longer, we believe in the war.

age, Gibbons knew how serious his wounds were by the look of horror that registered on the marine's face.

Despite these tribulations, the 6th Regiment quickly cleared the woods filled with Germans, then dueled the enemy in the streets of Bouresches. The fighting lasted into the night, but when June 7 dawned the village remained in American hands.

June 6 cost the marines dearly. By nightfall they had lost more than one thousand officers and men, more casualties than the Marine Corps had suffered in its entire history.

Because of a combination of General Pershing and Floyd Gibbons, who had written a highly flattering portrayal of the marines before traveling to the battlefield, the engagement at Belleau Wood became known as a marine affair, even though some French units and the U.S. Army had participated. Pershing permitted the press to give the lion's share of the reporting to the marines, and because few expected Gibbons to survive (he did), a military censor released—without changing a word—his prebattle account of the fighting.

Newspaper headlines in the United States trumpeted the victory. The *New York Times* reported that one could not go anywhere without hearing people talk about the marines at Belleau Wood, and marine recruiters noticed a decided increase in applicants.

The See-Saw Battle

For the remainder of June the marines and Germans waged almost constant battle, with first one side and then the other grabbing the upper hand. Men killed with rifles, machine guns, and bayonets, and when they

The marines suffered over a thousand casualties on June 6, more than in the entire prior existence of the Corps.

had no more bullets for their weapons, they turned to bare hands. Trees, denuded of their leaves and branches, stood like blackened toothpicks rising from ashes; shells and thousands of bullets stripped the bark off others. Belleau Wood, already clogged with dead branches, leaves, and brush, now filled with the grisly residue of warfare—discarded and unused rifles, helmets, mess kits, canteens, knapsacks, and letters from home —mingled with the dead.

Harbord ordered two other major assaults, one on June 8 and another on June 10, but neither succeeded in pushing the enemy out of their defenses. Each time the Americans rushed forward, the Germans shoved them back, then followed with their own assault across the wheat fields. In a fight that was typical of what occurred on a daily basis, moments before the Germans advanced, a sergeant named McCabe ran along the American line warning his men to shoot low into the wheat to better ensure a hit, then to be prepared for hand-to-hand

Blackened trees stood like toothpicks in Belleau Wood after a month of fighting between German troops and American marines.

combat. "Don't turn yellow and try to run," he warned his youthful charges. "If you do and the Germans don't kill you, I will."[61]

As the initial strains of daylight tried to break into dawn, the marines strained to see the Germans moving through the wheat field. Finally one man shouted, "Here they come!"[62] Three lines of Germans moved through the wheat in unison, bayonets glistening as daylight broke. Nervous marines held their fire as the enemy stepped nearer. After what seemed hours, the order to fire produced a sudden volley of gunfire that rattled across the landscape. Wheat stalks split in half and Germans fell, but more men took their place. With parched throats and dry mouths, McCabe's marines maintained their fire, sometimes shooting at such close range that they could easily see the look of stunned shock that registered on the faces of the German soldiers they hit.

The German line broke into smaller pockets, some moving toward the Americans and others hugging the ground before falling back. Ecstatic Americans cheered as the firing diminished, but they quickly forgot their jubilation to prepare for the inevitable next assault.

A dreary succession of attacks on both sides numbed men already exhausted of battle. Lacking food and supplies, some marines scavenged the pockets of dead bodies in search of food, but never could they have their fill. One said, "Food was not a problem. There just wasn't any during our first week in the wood."[63]

Don't Waste That Wine!

During the attack on Belleau Wood, as Lieutenant Clifton Cates headed across a wheat field toward Bouresches when a bullet smacked into his helmet and knocked him unconscious. When Cates awoke, he tried to put his helmet back on, but was unable because of a large dent in the headgear. Cates hastily sought shelter with four other marines. While they hugged the ground for protection, one of the marines poured some wine from his canteen into the damaged helmet and started pouring it over Cates's head. According to John Toland's *No Man's Land,* the officer shook his head and abruptly shouted, "God damn it, don't pour that wine over my head, give me a drink of it!" Cates took a deep swig of wine, then continued toward Bouresches.

Sometimes, Americans filtered into the woods, where they entered a strange new world where one could see hardly more than ten feet ahead through the dense forest. A soldier never knew if the next bush sheltered an enemy machine gun or if a German with a rifle hid in a nearby tree. In an attempt to gain a clearer view of the surrounding area, one American lieutenant climbed a tree. Within seconds he descended, exclaiming that a German machine gun nest sat mere yards from them.

The combat took such a heavy toll on marines that one battalion dropped from 1,000 men to only 350 in two weeks. When the wife of the commanding officer, Colonel Frederic M. Wise, asked in a letter how his men were doing, he wrote, "There aren't any more Marines."[64]

"They Lack Only Training and Experience"

A final June 25–26 American attack pushed the last Germans out of Belleau Wood and ended the fighting. The month-long strife cost almost ten thousand American casualties, but it proved that the newly formed army from across the ocean could mount an effective campaign against their more experienced foes. French military officials, who had earlier greeted the AEF with skepticism, swallowed their misgivings by awarding unit citations to the marines and renaming Belleau Wood the Wood of the Marine Brigade. They were now more

In this military cemetery adjacent to Belleau Wood, a sea of crosses stand as mute testimony to the human toll of the battle.

than happy to honor their allies, who could provide an almost unlimited pool of effective reinforcements to toss at the Germans.

On the other side of the line, the Germans viewed the results of Belleau Wood with alarm. If these initial troops performed so well, what would successive waves be like? German military leaders knew that 700,000 Americans had already arrived in France and that another 1 million would pour across the Atlantic within months. Their own resources and manpower would be sorely tested by fresh, vigorous forces at a time when fervor in Germany waned from four years of war.

An official report submitted shortly after the battle outlined the situation for Germany. The writers admired the American willingness to take heavy casualties and to attack with reckless abandon, and concluded:

> The different attacks on Belleau Wood were carried out with bravery and dash. The moral effect of our gunfire cannot seriously impede the advance of the American infantry. The Americans' nerves are not yet worn out. The qualities of the men individually may be described as remarkable. They are physically well set up, their attitude is good, and they range in age from eighteen to twenty-eight years. They lack at present only training and experience to make formidable adversaries. The men are in fine spirits and are filled with naive assurance; the words of a prisoner are characteristic—"We kill or we get killed."[65]

Many were killed. Almost twenty-three hundred American soldiers who fought at Belleau Wood lie in a war cemetery next to Belleau Wood, while another thousand rest elsewhere. Germany sacrificed more than eighty-six hundred soldiers attempting to hold on to the forest.

Those figures say nothing of the numerous men on both sides who suffered wounds. Pershing received firsthand evidence of injuries when he visited a hospital filled with Americans and saw the victims of gas attacks and enemy bullets. Their courage moved the commander even more. As he wandered from bed to bed to speak to the men, those physically able enough stood to salute, even those who had been blinded by gas attacks. They struggled to their feet, bandages covering their eyes, and snapped a crisp salute to their commanding officer.

The most touching moment occurred when Pershing walked to the bed of a soldier named Jimmy, who had lost his right arm in the fighting. The youth whispered an apology for not being able to salute, but an obviously emotional Pershing brushed his hand through the boy's hair and replied, "No, it's I that should salute you."[66]

Pershing had not only triumphed on the battlefield, but he had also won favor in the United States, France, and Germany. By wresting a sturdy defensive position from some of the finest troops in Europe, he proved that these brash young Americans could fight. They would not simply be fodder to be thrown into slaughter—they would be the anchor upon which peace could be solidified.

Chapter 6

Saint-Mihiel

The brash young American officer stood in the middle of No-Man's-Land tapping the wet ground with his feet. He had heard that this marshy area, further dampened by recent rains, would be too soft for his tank unit to take part in the upcoming offensive.

Lieutenant Colonel George Patton was determined, though, that he would be right in the middle of action when the shells started flying, so he wanted to see for himself if the land could support the tanks he commanded. One look convinced him that the ground, although soggy, would be firm enough.

Something about the patrol bothered him, though: The French and German soldiers in this sector seemed unwilling to fight each other. As they quietly approached German lines, Patton was stunned to hear the Germans whistle to the French squad, and the French whistle a reply. When he asked what was happening, a French officer replied, "The whistle meant that if the raid had been pushed further the Germans would reluctantly be forced to fire."[67]

Patton returned to his lines, annoyed that soldiers would be so reluctant to fight. But he took solace in the knowledge that this would soon change, for in a few days the long-awaited first all-American offensive of the war would transform the relatively peaceful Saint-Mihiel sector into one of action and noise.

"An Independent American Army"

Saint-Mihiel is located in the northeast portion of France, 150 miles east of Paris and 20 miles from the German border. Because it stood so close to Germany, Saint-Mihiel was one of the first French towns to fall to the kaiser's invading armies in 1914, and the town had remained in German hands ever since. The Germans held a line stretching from the Côtes-de-Meuse hills on the western side of the sector to the heights of Montsec and Loupmont on the southern front, forming a 15-square-mile triangular bulge, or salient, in the Allied line. This salient severed important Allied communications lines, and Allied leaders hoped an offensive would eliminate the German presence.

In the middle of the sector is the crater-pocked Woevre Plain. The flat land of the Woevre invited an assault, but obstacles existed as well. Rivers and streams dissected the plain and heavy rain turned the area into an almost impassable swamp because its clay-like soil would not soak up the water.

Because the region had received substantial amounts of rain in the two weeks before the assault, the German task of defending the sector would be easier. Allied

Lieutenant Colonel George Patton was sure that his tanks could trek through the wet ground of No-Man's-Land.

tanks would run into trouble once they tried to roll across the drenched ground. The Germans added a few twists of their own to augment nature, including miles of barbed wire, hundreds of machine gun posts, and numerous trenches. They placed artillery units on surrounding heights to ensure that a constant stream of lethal gunfire descended on an invading force.

General John J. Pershing, commander of American troops, called the Saint-Mihiel salient an indomitable field fortress. Soldiers preparing for the attack knew that in 1915, their French allies had left sixty thou-

The Germans placed artillery units on the high ground surrounding Woevre Plain. A night-time barrage shows the gun crews in stark relief.

sand casualties lying on the field vainly trying to take this same area.

Pershing could list any number of military reasons for unleashing the Saint-Mihiel attack. A successful campaign would remove German artillery as a threat; restore severed lines of communications; cut German railway lines, thereby hampering the enemy's abilities to respond to Allied threats elsewhere; and endanger the vital German Saar region, long a major supplier of weapons, coal, and iron.

Behind these reasons lay a deeper, emotional issue. Since the first American soldiers arrived in France in 1917, they had fought in every major western European land conflict. They had never, however, battled as an independent unit, but had always been placed on the line under the control of another nation's commander. Pershing longed to change this. Saint-Mihiel would be America's, an assault that soldiers on the front lines and civilians back home could call their own.

Before Pershing could launch his attack against the Germans, he had to fight a verbal battle with his French allies, who favored retaining American units under their control. Pershing faced a powerful opponent in the Allied supreme commander, France's Ferdinand Foch. The French commander wanted to incorporate the U.S. soldiers into a British assault, with which Pershing adamantly disagreed. When Foch pressed the issue Pershing replied,

Marshal Foch, you have no authority as Allied Commander-in-Chief to call upon me to yield up my command of the American Army and have it scattered among the Allied forces where it will not be an American army at all. While our army will fight wherever you may decide, it will not fight except as an independent American army.[68]

By now Foch realized little would be accomplished in this stubborn standoff. He agreed to compromise: Pershing could have his all-American offensive at Saint-Mihiel only if he agreed to transport his army to the Meuse-Argonne sector in time for the wider attack scheduled in two weeks. Pershing knew that the intricacies of moving a vast number of men from one sector to another would be immense, but to obtain the offensive he wanted, he readily assented.

Colonel George C. Marshall, who would play a prominent role in World War II as head of all American military forces, prepared a simple battle plan. A main thrust would smash into the German southern flank and push north, where it would join with another force that had attacked from the west, thereby trapping the Germans.

American forces outnumbered their German foe two to one, with 665,000 men in nineteen divisions. An impressive array of 3,200 guns, 265 tanks, and an astounding 1,476 airplanes under the command of Colonel Billy Mitchell stood ready to assist.

German general Max von Gallwitz planned to harass the Americans in the Saint-Mihiel salient with sacrificial machine gun squads, then hastily pull back to the

stronger Hindenburg Line. He hoped to weaken American resolve in this manner, but Gallwitz underestimated his opponents' ability to attack quickly and with many troops.

American troops, here on their way to the Saint-Mihiel front, had been under the command of other nations' military leaders since joining the fight.

A Ruse in Belfort

This German underestimation came, in part, because of some slick deception by Pershing. Wishing to take no chances on losing this first all-American assault, Pershing dispatched the commander of VIII Corps, Major Omar Bundy, to the town of Belfort, near the Swiss border. Pershing knew that Belfort housed spies from all sides

trying to pick up information on their enemies. He ordered Major Bundy and his men to check into the Grand Hotel Du Tonneau d'Or and begin openly drawing plans for an American attack through the Belfort Gap, far from the action at Saint-Mihiel. Bundy even left the paper shreds detailing the offensive in his wastebasket, knowing that Germans would bribe hotel waiters and chambermaids for this information. It was not long before plans of the American "attack" through the Belfort Gap were in German hands. The German High Command, although knowing America would strike somewhere near Saint-Mihiel, believed it could not ignore this information and switched some troops from the Saint-Mihiel sector to guard the Belfort area.

Just how much the German High Command was fooled by Pershing's scheme is hard to measure. The Germans possessed a clear view of the surrounding terrain from Montsec, which rose 450 feet above the Woevre Plain. On September 8 the Germans floated a balloon carrying a message across to American lines warning that they knew the Americans would soon attack and that they were ready for them. Some German troops were moved from the Saint-Mihiel area, but according to American pilot Eddie Rickenbacker, everyone in Paris knew all about the Saint-Mihiel assault.

Every taxi driver or waiter in Paris could have told one just where the other Americans were concentrating for their great attack on the St. Mihiel salient. The number of guns, the number of troops and just where they were located, were discussed by every man on the streets.[69]

Eddie Rickenbacker

Eddie Rickenbacker, the aviator who shot down more enemy planes than any other American, was born in Ohio in 1890. He developed a deep love for machines as a youth and raced cars before the war. After flight school the talented Rickenbacker assumed command of the 94th Aero Pursuit Squadron, then proceeded to shoot down twenty-six German aircraft and observation balloons. On September 25, 1918, he earned the Congressional Medal of Honor by single-handedly attacking seven enemy airplanes and shooting down two.

After the war he served as president of Eastern Airlines and performed special assignments for the Army air forces. Rickenbacker died in 1973.

Eddie Rickenbacker shot down more enemy planes than any other American during World War I

Pershing's ruse may not have helped much, but it shows the concern he carried that American troops win a resounding victory at Saint-Mihiel. As doughboys (American infantrymen) gathered at their jump-off areas and as tanks rolled toward Saint-Mihiel, Pershing knew that American honor demanded a stunning success.

"Go Forward"

American soldiers began quietly preparing for battle in the early morning hours of September 12. Each man received two extra bandoleers (strings) of ammunition to drape about their necks, then officers raced among their men checking and rechecking that they carried the required grenades, entrenching tools, first aid kits, food, and water. The somber mood surrounding men who were about to go into battle was dampened by the uncooperative fog and heavy rain. Footing would be treacherous; progress slow.

The man whose tanks would be most affected by the miserable conditions—George Patton—readied himself for battle in two very different ways. The night before the attack, Patton had been cited for a Distinguished Service Order for personally reconnoitering a bridge—reported to be mined—that his tanks were to use. He wanted his officers to act the same way and exhorted them to constantly

Go forward, go forward. If your tank breaks down go forward with the Infantry. . . . If you are left alone in the midst of the enemy keep shooting. If your gun is disabled use your pistols and squash the enemy with your tracks . . . you are the first American tanks [in battle]. You must establish the fact that AMERICAN TANKS DO NOT SURRENDER.[70]

He ended his orders by threatening to shoot any officer he found behind the front line of infantry.

After issuing these harsh edicts, Patton sat down to write his daily letter to his wife, Bea. Using words his threatened officers would find hard to believe, he assured his wife she could rest easy because he was fully prepared for battle and had put on clean underwear.

American artillery erupted at 1:00 A.M., shattering the still silence and turning the darkness into an eerie light. For four hours, American artillery smashed German machine gun nests and emplacements. Major Frederick Palmer, a press relations officer, described the incredible shelling as "A man-made aurora borealis shot out of the darkness. . . . All the world, enclosed under canopy of night, was aflame."[71]

At 5:00 A.M. the troops climbed over the parapets (low walls) and attacked behind a rolling barrage. The first man out of the trenches for the 84th Brigade of the Rainbow Division was Douglas MacArthur, who wanted to set an example for his men. It seems he had extra incentive for quickly abandoning his headquarters. All night long his command post had been bombarded by heavy shelling. MacArthur could not figure out why his headquarters received such attention when other areas went virtually untouched. It was not until after the battle that MacArthur learned the answer from a captured German map. Neatly penciled in on the map was the precise location of MacArthur's headquarters.

General Pershing watched the battle's progress, content that his American Army had finally engaged the enemy on its own terms but concerned for the safety of the men he sent into battle.

> The exultation in our minds that here, at last, after seventeen months of effort, an American army was fighting under its own flag was tempered by the realization of the sacrifice of life on both sides, and yet fate willed it thus and we must carry it through.[72]

American troops encountered light resistance in most areas since German soldiers were in the process of pulling back to new lines when the assault began. On the western side of the attack the U.S. I Corps charged ahead after a forty-minute smoke screen and advanced so quickly they captured many Germans still in their dugouts. By noon, after a bitter battle with machine gun nests in a gas-filled valley, the I Corps achieved its main objectives for the first day.

The IV Corps faced tougher opposition on the southern side but it, too, accomplished its first day's objectives quickly. Some units captured its second day's objectives by

Douglas MacArthur set an example for his men by being the first one out of the trenches when his brigade was fired upon.

nightfall of the first day, while MacArthur's men advanced an astonishing five miles in the initial day.

The German Retreat

The swiftness of the American attack took the German leaders by surprise. They had grown accustomed to methodical British and French advances but here, all of a sudden, came wildly attacking doughboys who rarely stopped to regroup. The Germans were completely confused with the unconventional fighting tactics used by these "cowboy" Americans, as they called them.

Instead of the precise frontal assaults used by British and French troops, the Americans employed frontier-style methods. From his lofty position in the air, Captain Eddie Rickenbacker watched his countrymen baffle the Germans and compared them to Indians.

They scurried from cover to cover, always crouching low as they ran. Throwing themselves flat they would get their rifles into action and spray the Boches with more bullets until they withdrew from sight. Then another running advance and another furious pumping of lead from the Yanks.[73]

German soldiers, too, compared the Americans to Indians and feared that they might be scalped if captured.

The rapid American advance led to some strange sights. MacArthur and his men stormed into the French town of Essey with such swiftness that his men had difficulty making the townspeople believe they were Americans. Once the townspeople realized who these soldiers were, they warmly welcomed their liberators and went into their homes to take out small American flags. Because the flags had been copied from newspaper pictures, the Americans were greeted by black-and-white American flags. On the second day, MacArthur's men almost captured intact the headquarters of

the 19th German Army Corps. "Amongst many other evidences of their hasty departure," wrote MacArthur after the battle, "we found a fully set dining room table, and a prepared meal."[74]

The men of Corporal Alvin York's battalion were upset that the Germans were falling back and "cussed the Germans out for not standing and they kept yelling at them to wait and fight it out." York, who

Corporal Alvin York had trouble keeping up with the men he had to lead because they were so eager to defeat the Germans.

would later emerge as one of the war's biggest heroes, found himself struggling to keep up with the men he was supposed to lead because "no matter how fast I went they wanted to go faster, so . . . they could get the Germans."[75]

The quick advance caused problems for some American units. Support services had trouble keeping up and even forced German prisoners, including white-gloved officers, to carry wounded away from the battle. One soldier recalled that they were moving so quickly they did not have time to guard German prisoners. They disarmed the enemy and sent them away.

The battle at Saint-Mihiel was the last time the U.S. Cavalry was used in combat.

Old and New Cavalry

In one of history's ironies, two weapons noted for quickness saw service at Saint-Mihiel—one an old, established method seeing its last use in battle; the other a new concept that would quickly replace the older manner of warfare. Pershing dispatched two hundred mounted cavalry to pursue the fleeing Germans. According to one historian, the mere sight of the horses must have reinforced in German minds the image of wild frontier Americans. This attack was the final time the U.S. Cavalry, which had been so instrumental in the Civil War and the elimination of the American Indian, played a role in battle.

While the romantic cavalry limped off the stage of American military history, its replacement—the tank—moved onto center stage. Saint-Mihiel was the first action seen by the new American Tank Corps, and in spite of Patton's stern commands, it did little better than the cavalry because of mud, mechanical problems, inavailability of gasoline, and inexperience.

Patton roamed the front lines, prodding his tanks forward and looking for likely avenues of advance. When a tank became mired in the mud, Patton rushed over to arrange for its removal. The energetic commander seemed to be everywhere. He once spotted a man in a shell hole holding onto his rifle but not firing at the enemy. An irritated Patton hastened over to bully the man to action, but stopped short when he saw a bullet hole through his forehead.

He moved on to another tank that had halted. When he questioned its commander, Patton realized the man and his crew, manning the only tank in sight, hesitated at advancing so close to German lines. To calm their nerves, Patton offered to sit on top of the vehicle while it moved forward. Showing no apprehension—yet filled inside with dread—Patton mounted the tank and rode ahead. His actions gained the admiration of the tank crew and the accompanying infantry.

While at the front, Patton had a chance meeting with Douglas MacArthur that could have been far more disastrous than anything experienced by his tanks. Shells exploded all around the two as they talked, but neither man wanted to be the first to seek shelter. Instead of taking cover, the two proud leaders chatted with each other in the open as a creeping barrage slowly approached.

Patton recalled that "each one wanted to leave but each hated to say so, so we let it [the creeping barrage] come over to us."[76] Fortunately neither man was injured in this egotistic episode. However, a properly placed German shell in World War I could have had alarming repercussions for Germany, Japan, and the United States in World War II when both men would reach fame as two of that war's most prominent generals.

"A Strange Feeling of Dread"

Action also filled the skies above Saint-Mihiel. Colonel Billy Mitchell used his large air force as an offensive arm. Although weather hampered his operations the first day, planes began sorties by noon, and for the next three days his fliers bombed and strafed German lines and provided reconnaissance

The Neel Brothers

Flying above Saint-Mihiel was Second Lieutenant Roland H. Neel, aerial observer of the 99th Aero Squadron, who one month earlier had been awarded the Distinguished Service Order for attacking Germans even after his control wires had been shot away. While Roland prowled the skies his brother, acting Captain Joseph Neel, led a charge of E Company of the 327th Infantry. On the first day of battle serious wounds slowed him down, but he refused to go to the hospital. Instead, Joseph Neel led a large reconnaissance force that ran into stiff opposition. Of six officers and 252 men in his company, only 72 returned, including Joseph Neel. The captain, though, lay on a stretcher with a mortal blow to the head, which caused his death two days later.

for ground troops. Aviator Harold Buckley flew as low as fifty feet above enemy lines, splattering German trenches with machine gun bullets and shooting up troop trains, supply vehicles, and any other available target.

Eddie Rickenbacker and another American flier, Reed Chambers, harassed the Germans all day. Sighting a long column of German soldiers with three-inch guns slowly winding along a road, Rickenbacker and Chambers swooped down on the Germans and

> All down the line we continued our fire. The whole column was thrown into the wildest confusion. Horses plunged and broke away. Some were killed and fell in their tracks. Most of the drivers and gunners had taken to the trees before we reached them.[77]

The second day tossed more challenges Rickenbacker's way. Early in the day he sighted four German Fokker D-7's chasing American planes. The American ace climbed to position with the sun at his back, let the four Germans pass below him, then attacked. He dove on the last one, sending it smoking to the ground with short bursts from his machine gun. Instantly, however, the other three German planes turned on Rickenbacker and "I found myself staring full into three beautiful scarlet noses headed straight in my direction. . . . I had blundered single-handed into the Richthofen crowd!"[78]

Rickenbacker was being pursued by members of the legendary Manfred von Richthofen's Flying Circus. Although the famous Red Baron had been killed earlier in the war, his fellow fliers were just as aggressive and Rickenbacker had to employ every ounce of his considerable skill to evade death.

Rickenbacker eluded his skillful pursuers, and the next day shot down his seventh plane, making him the "American Ace of Aces"—the one pilot with the most kills. Although it was an honor, Rickenbacker was not sure if it was one he wanted. "It was an honor for which I had risked my life many times, but I had a strange feeling of dread. Four other fliers had held that title. All were dead."[79]

Lieutenant Sumner Sewell had a different type of experience in the air. His plane caught on fire after being riddled by bullets from a pursuing German plane. The German followed for awhile, but as Sewell neared the ground the attacker left, believing Sewell was about to crash. By this time the flames in Sewell's plane had gone out so Sewell crash landed in a shell hole. As he crawled out from his wreckage, shaken but safe, a falling object smacked into the ground a few feet away from him. It was one of the wheels to his plane that had been shot off in the aerial dogfight. After surviving a ferocious skirmish, and a terrifying dive, Sewell was nearly killed by his own wheel.

Mitchell's air force at Saint-Mihiel was far from the future massed air squadrons of World War II. As Eddie Rickenbacker wrote

In this recreation, Eddie Rickenbacker and another pilot face three Fokker D-7's that are diving towards them.

of Saint-Mihiel, though, for the first time in history the U.S. Air Service "played a major role in a major campaign. Air power had wrought damage on and behind the lines, but, equally important, it had destroyed the morale of the enemy as well."[80]

An All-American Victory

The American advance on land continued to progress swiftly, in part because they had caught the Germans while they were pulling back. When Pershing realized what was happening, he ordered the IV and V Corps to move through the night toward the town of Vigneulles and seal off the German escape route. By 8:00 A.M. the next morning, the American units met at the French town. Later in the day the First Army pushed up to meet the new American line at Vigneulles and eliminated the Saint-Mihiel salient. For all practical purposes the battle was over, giving Pershing two reasons to celebrate. This day—September 13—was also his fifty-eighth birthday.

Pershing's all-American army had achieved a resounding success at Saint-Mihiel. Congratulations quickly poured into Pershing's headquarters from President Woodrow Wilson and French leader Georges Clemenceau. Foch telegraphed that the United States "has won a magnificent victory by a maneuver as skillfully prepared as it was valiantly executed."[81] Most

Allied leaders believed Saint-Mihiel gave French morale a much-needed boost while it gave Germany, which had doubted American ability to assemble an effective army, a large shock. Erich Ludendorff, a German general, reportedly reacted with such stunned disbelief that aides wondered if he could continue to command.

Pershing's forces liberated two hundred square miles of French territory in the Saint-Mihiel drive. Fifteen thousand German soldiers and 257 German guns were captured by the swift-moving Americans, for a price that was considered relatively light in a war whose battles mangled bodies by the thousands. In two days, seven thousand Americans became casualties, one-third the number expected by the Medical Corps, which had prepared sixty hospital trains and twenty-two thousand hospital beds for Saint-Mihiel.

The battle of Saint-Mihiel was not one of the epic battles fought in World War I. But for Pershing and for the American people, Saint-Mihiel was memorable because for the first time, America had fielded an all-American army and had successfully engaged the enemy. Pershing would later claim, "This striking victory completely demonstrated the wisdom of building up a distinct American army."[82] Pershing, and America, had a victory they could call their own.

Chapter 7

The Siegfried Line: Germany's Last Defense

One final battle remained before the long, weary war ended. Though stricken with supply difficulties, the Germans counted on their experienced soldiers, protected by sturdy defenses, to repel any Allied attempt to seize ground. The Allies, on the other hand, readied a powerful strike to finally break through the vaunted German defense lines.

"Everyone in the Fight"

France's Ferdinand Foch crafted a plan that he hoped would so severely interrupt the flow of supplies pouring out of Germany to its soldiers along the western front that the Germans would ask for peace. His three-part assault called for a main advance to occur about eighty miles northeast of Paris. In the middle, American soldiers would penetrate the German lines in the dense Argonne Forest and take the railway junction at Mézières, while a second cleared the heights along the Meuse River to the east and the third outflanked the Germans on the Aisne River to the west. At the same time, British and French units all along the western front would launch attacks to apply pressure in so many different locations that Germany would be hard pressed to dispatch reinforcements to any locale. Foch's cry of "Everyone in the fight"[83] brought 160 Allied divisions into the attack, supported by another 60 in reserve.

Foch faced formidable problems. He wanted to punch through the opposition line before Germany could rush in reinforcements, but his men and supplies could move along only three railway lines and three narrow roads pocketed with thousands of shell holes. This might be sufficient for a smaller action, but Foch's 600,000 soldiers had difficulty simply arriving at the front in time for the jump-off. Thousands of horses labored along the roads, which were transformed into muddy quagmires by heavy rains, to bring men and supplies forward, many dying in the effort.

weapons. Veterans took advantage by charging $5 to show these green troops the proper method.

The Germans placed 113 divisions, backed by another 84 in reserve, along the sturdy Siegfried Line, a series of four defensive barriers ranging from three to twenty miles in depth. With typical thoroughness, the Germans combined nature with military craftiness to fashion an imposing complex of fortifications. To the east of the Meuse River, along the steep Côtes-de-Meuse, they placed artillery guns that could blanket the regions below with deadly fire. Farther to the west, they strung thousands of miles of barbed wire and entrenched hundreds of machine gun posts in the Argonne Forest, while numerous ridges and hills offered superb positions for German defenders while funneling Allied troops into lower lands below. Particularly formidable was Montfaucon, a German-held hill dominating the midsection of the defenses. The area had been so heavily fortified by the Germans that Foch had avoided sending his own French soldiers into this region for four years. It would be up to the largely untested American Army to take such a forbidding place.

Shortly before the attack opened, American major general Robert Alexander, commander of the 77th Division, briefed his officers in the presence of a French officer. The Frenchman remained silent while Alexander explained details of the plan one final time, but when the subordinate officers left, the Frenchman turned to Alexander and said,

Field Marshal Ferdinand Foch devised a plan that would cut off German soldiers' supplies so critically that Germany would ask for peace.

Because the offensive at Saint-Mihiel tied down so many troops General Pershing, in command of the American troops who would do the bulk of the fighting in the Argonne Forest region, had to place inexperienced men in the lines to ensure he had sufficient numbers to open an attack. Some Americans had been drafted less than three months earlier and did not even know how to properly insert rifle clips into their

Sir, I have no doubt that your men are brave and that you have made every preparation that will give them a chance for victory tomorrow, but permit me to say that, in my opinion, the line in your front will not move. It has been in place for four years, is solidly established, well wired in, and the German is a good soldier. I fear that you will not be able to make the advance you hope for."[84]

Alexander patiently listened, then curtly replied, "The line *will* move."[84]

Though facing a daunting task, Pershing exuded confidence that his men would suc-ceed. His men may have been inexperienced, but they had not been worn down from three years of fighting in Europe as other nations' soldiers had. He believed their morale would overcome their shortcomings. He told a fellow officer, "In my opinion no other Allied troops had the morale or offensive spirit to overcome successfully the difficulties to be met in the Meuse-Argonne sector."[85]

The formidable German Siegfried Line, comprised of numerous fortifications, intimidated the French for years. It was left to the U.S. Army to attack and breach the line.

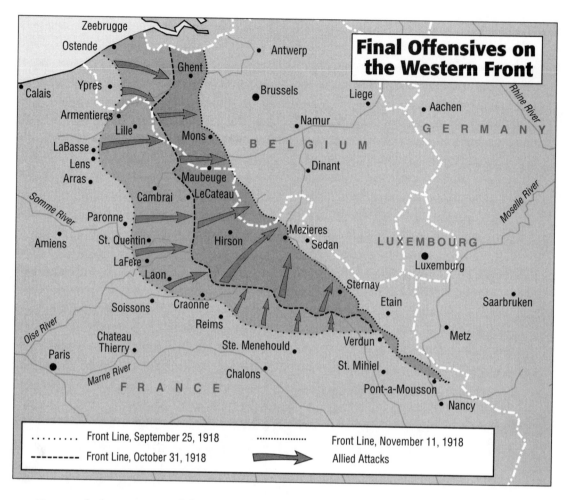

Final Offensives on the Western Front

.... Front Line, September 25, 1918 ················· Front Line, November 11, 1918

--------- Front Line, October 31, 1918 ➡ Allied Attacks

Toward the Immovable Line

As the offensive neared, Pershing's men prepared in different ways. Artillery Captain Harry S. Truman, future president of the United States, stayed up all night to verify his calculations for the coming barrage. In his typically imperfect grammar, Lieutenant Colonel George Patton wrote his wife, Bea:

Just a word to you before I leave to play a part in what promises to be the biggest

battle of the war or world so far. I am always nervous about this time just as at Polo or Football before the game starts but so far I have been all right after that. I hope I keep on that way it is more pleasant. [86]

A thundering barrage opened the attack at 2:30 A.M. on September 26, 1918. In three hours Truman and other artillerymen boomed 4.2 million shells across to the German lines, more ammunition than was used in the entire Civil War by both sides. Lieutenant General Robert Lee Bullard compared the sound of the barrage to

> the collision of a million express trains. Besides the noise there was the feel of concussion, quivering ground—and that inevitable wait, while officers scanned luminous watch faces, and engineers and sergeants gazed at compasses with which, by dead reckoning, they were to lead through a No Man's Land where past shell fire and present fog eliminated landmarks.[87]

As the first of the six hundred thousand troops stepped to the jump-off line and collected the inner strength to head toward the enemy, Captain Eddie Rickenbacker, the United States' most renowned aviator, flew above as part of the air umbrella provided by eight hundred Allied aircraft. The impressive artillery display created an eerie presence. "Through the darkness the whole western horizon was illumined with one mass of jagged flashes. The picture made me think of a giant switchboard which emitted thousands of electric flashes as invisible hands manipulated the plugs."[88]

At 5:30 A.M. a rolling barrage replaced the thundering bombardment and young American soldiers emerged from their trenches. In one location, as the men of the 165th Infantry stepped out, the unit chaplain, Father Duffy, blessed them from a hill. All along the line the inexperienced troops moved with a confidence that comes from ignorance, for they had no idea what lay ahead. "All these things added to nervous force," wrote Brigadier General James Harbord, "energy without limit, confidence, youth and optimism—we were substituting for experience."[89]

The untested American soldiers made impressive initial gains in the middle before being halted by the Germans. They advanced three miles into enemy territory and seized Montfaucon, but a speedy German counterthrust resulted in surrounding the Americans. For the next three days they battled without reinforcements, as food and water supplies dwindled.

Behind the lines, Truman directed his artillery with gusto. One soldier reported

Harry S. Truman was an artillery captain during World War I.

that the future president stood in the midst of his men, "his tin hat pushed on the back of his head, directing salvos. He was a banty officer in spectacles, runnin' and cussin' all at the same time. I never heard a man cuss so well or so intelligently."[90]

Patton led the way for his 142 American tanks by standing in the open and, like a police officer directing a flow of traffic around the scene of an accident, shouting at his men to veer one way or the other. When a group of soldiers begged him to seek shelter from the German shells and bullets that smacked dangerously close to the officer, Patton abruptly replied, "To Hell with them—they can't hit me."[91]

The bravado impressed the men, but not the Germans. A bullet that passed through Patton's upper left thigh and emerged from his buttocks removed the aggressive Patton from battle.

Captain Eddie Rickenbacker attacked observation balloons sent aloft by the Germans and searched in the darkness for enemy aircraft. One opponent challenged Rickenbacker, and the two engaged in a gunfight that lit the skies. Tracer bullets— ammunition that purposely glowed as it moved toward the target to indicate the proximity of the shot to the target—sped from one to the other craft as both men anxiously tried to best his foe. The aviator, who shot down twenty-six German aircraft by war's end, later recalled, "For a moment it looked as though our two machines were tied together with four ropes of fire (two machine guns from each aircraft)."[92]

Despite the impressive initial showing, which gained more ground compared to other offensives along the western front, the American attack slowed in the face of increased enemy opposition. Some units moved as far as seven miles, while others hammered futilely against the German lines without making progress. By the second day a combination of swift German reaction and ineffective American response halted the drive by October 1.

Though the Americans captured ten thousand German soldiers in fewer than four days, they had not ousted the enemy from its positions in the Meuse-Argonne. Critics, especially in the French Army, called for Pershing's removal, but General Foch dismissed the attacks on the grounds that the Americans, like the French and British before them, needed time to learn how to fight under the deplorable conditions along the western front. Pershing remained in command of his American Army and would coordinate the Meuse-Argonne drive until war's end. Happily for those involved, only six weeks of strife lay ahead before the final gun sounded.

The Forest of Perpetual Gloom

During the first week of October the Allies halted along the Meuse-Argonne to reorganize lines and prepare for the next phase. Foch, who had defended the Americans against angry critics, met with Pershing to remind him that, while the fighting in his sector might be arduous and the terrain near impassable, "I only consider results."[93]

George S. Patton

George Strong Patton Jr. was born in California in 1885. He graduated from the military academy at West Point in 1909, then served with the American expedition into Mexico led by General John J. Pershing. His service gained the attention of Pershing, who brought Patton with him when he headed to France as commander of the American Expeditionary Force. The aggressive young officer hoped for combat, though, and besieged his superior with requests for transfer to the infantry. In November 1917 he received his wish and joined the U.S. Tank Corps.

The next August he led the tanks into battle at Saint-Mihiel, then followed with more action the next month in the Argonne offensive. His experience with tanks gained Patton a reputation as a rising officer and an expert on the new vehicles.

Following his distinguished record in World War I, Patton touted the benefits of mechanized warfare, as epitomized by the tank. When the December 7, 1941, Japanese attack on Pearl Harbor dragged the United States into World War II, Patton commanded an armored corps and played a major role in the North African and Sicilian campaigns. His major contribution came in the drive across France in 1944, when his tanks smashed through German lines and sped toward Germany.

The outspoken Patton seemed to be constantly in hot water with superiors. The most infamous episode occurred in 1943 when, during a visit to a hospital, he slapped a soldier suffering from battle fatigue and called him a coward. Only his reputation as an outstanding commander saved Patton from being sent home in disgrace, although he was temporarily removed from command.

After orchestrating the dash through France and witnessing the end to World War II, Patton was mortally injured in a December 9, 1945, car accident, one day before he was scheduled to leave Europe for home. He died twelve days later from a broken neck.

Pershing scheduled October 4 as the date for the second major attack. While fighting occurred all along the line, the major thrust occurred in the Argonne Forest, a thick growth of thousands of trees cut by streams and ridges. Historian S. L. A. Marshall described it as

Hard-rock-bedded, slashed through by intersecting ravines, the Argonne is wrapped in perpetual gloom. Guns and heavy trucks can't traverse it. Within it, a soldier's horizon is limited to grenade range. Units found their way by guess or dead reckoning. The enemy had every trail covered and every height crowned by a machine gun nest. [94]

Hoping to surprise the Germans, Pershing sent his men out of the trenches without the usual preinvasion bombardment. The Americans carefully advanced in the mist and fog of October 4 until they drew within fifty yards, when chaos erupted. Private First Class James Rose recalled,

The air about us became a solid sheet of machine-gun and heavy artillery fire. No words could possibly describe the horror of it. Body stacked upon body in waves and piles, and the whole bloody massacre was made vividly clear to the rest of us by continuous flashes of gun-fire from the entrenched line of German machine guns. Our boys never faltered, they came,

wave on wave, climbing over the bodies of their fallen comrades with one obsession in their minds, to reach and destroy every machine gun which was mowing down our advance. Heroes all of them.[95]

American infantry assaulted different sectors of the German lines to locate an opening. Repulsed in some with heavy losses, they gained yards in others. One group of soldiers came upon a series of German blockhouses with large underground recreation centers, complete with libraries, pool tables, music rooms, and bars.

A position not far away offered a different story. German troops entrenched on the Côte de Châtillon, a razor-backed ridge, repelled each American attempt to seize the ridge. Finally, General Charles P. Summerall

Shot in the throat, an American soldier collapses as his unit continues its advance toward the German line.

contacted the commanding officer of the 84th Infantry Brigade, Colonel Douglas MacArthur, and ordered him to "Give me Châtillon or a list of 5,000 casualties."[96] MacArthur wanted to protest because he knew that Summerall did not appreciate the difficulty of the assignment, but he assented and told his superior he would either take the ridge or his own name would be first on the list of deaths.

MacArthur led his men toward the Germans amidst shellfire and screams. He later wrote that so many officers died that sergeants replaced them on the battlefield, and that corporals assumed command of companies. By the time he seized the Côte de Châtillon, one major reported only three hundred men and six officers surviving out of one thousand four hundred and fifty.

In many instances the courageous action of one individual stirred the others to gallantry. Private Rose's superior, Lieutenant Parker, rushed directly at a German machine gun nest, grabbed the hot gun barrel and hurled it into the woods as the Germans surrendered. Inspired by this display of bravery, the other men jumped into the German trenches and ripped the rifles out of their enemies' hands.

Captain Frank Williams's feat impressed every onlooker. A quick-draw artist from the West who had appeared in numerous Wild West shows, Williams scouted a hill one morning and spotted five rifle-toting Germans taking one American prisoner away. Williams casually walked toward the Germans, who did not immediately fire because they noticed the American's pistol was still in its holder. When the captain drew close enough, with lightning speed he drew the gun and shot four Germans before any could even raise their rifles. The fifth wisely surrendered.

Corporal Alvin York provided the most amazing individual story to emerge from the Argonne. On October 8, York, a sharpshooter who honed his skills hunting turkeys in the mountains of Tennessee, moved through a valley with his unit when the Germans struck from both sides. "Our boys just went down like the long grass before the mowing machine at home," York later wrote. He and sixteen men tried to move around the side to eliminate the machine guns, but German fire killed six and wounded three more before they moved within range.

Huddling close to the ground, York put his shooting prowess to work. He waited until a German head peeked above the trench line, then fired. One by one, he picked off opposing soldiers like shooting turkeys at home.

> I don't think I missed a shot. It was no time to miss. In order to sight me or to swing their machine guns on me, the Germans had to show their heads above the trench, and every time I saw a head I just touched it off. All the time I kept yelling at them to come down [and surrender]. I didn't want to kill any more than I had to. But it was they or I. And I was giving them the best I had. Suddenly a German officer and five men jumped out of the trench and charged me with fixed bayonets. I changed to the old automatic and just touched them off too. I touched off the sixth man first, then the fifth, then the fourth, then the third, and so on. I wanted them to keep coming. I didn't want the rear ones to see me touching off the front ones, I was afraid they would drop down and pump a volley into me.[97]

York killed more than twenty Germans before a major surrendered to him. Holding a gun to the officer's head, York entered the

German lines and bluffed other enemy soldiers into laying down their weapons. He and the other seven Americans who accompanied him then marched their prisoners—an astounding 132—back to American lines. For his deeds, which included knocking out 35 German machine guns, York was promoted to sergeant and received the Congressional Medal of Honor.

The Lost Battalion

The saga written in the Argonne Forest has one more incredible chapter. Major Charles W. Whittlesey, commander of the 1st Battalion of the 308th Infantry Regiment, 77th Division, and Captain George C. McMurtry, commander of the 2nd Battalion, became trapped in heavy fighting along a winding road on the slope of a ravine. German grenades tumbled down the steep incline

Alvin York single-handedly captured one hundred and thirty-two German soldiers at the battle at the Argonne Forest.

into their midst, and as the fighting ensued the surrounded Americans became so short on supplies that they had to take bandages from the dead to reuse on the freshly wounded. Whittlesey sent carrier pigeons with the message, "Men are suffering from hunger and exposure; and the wounded are in very bad condition. Cannot support be sent at once?"[98] Other Americans tried to help the trapped men, but in the dense Argonne Forest swarming with enemy soldiers, their lines could not be located.

At one point a flurry of American shells burst near their position, then began creeping toward the besieged Americans. Whittlesey calmed the men by shouting encouragement that the barrage would not last long, but the shells ripped into the soldiers' ranks and killed eighty men. One shell directly hit Whittlesey's orderly, Sergeant Major Ben Gaedeke, who disintegrated in a thunderous explosion.

With hope running out, Whittlesey attached a plea to his final carrier pigeon, a bird called Cher Ami. When the pigeon landed on a branch instead of flying toward headquarters, Americans shouted and hurled sticks at it in an effort to start it on its way, but Cher Ami held its ground. Finally, one man climbed the tree, shook the branch, and prodded the reluctant Cher Ami into flight.

German soldiers, knowing the animal contained a message that might bring reinforcements, shot at Cher Ami, but it escaped with only a slightly injured leg. It flew to headquarters, plummeted to the ground, stumbled about as if dazed, then hopped on one leg to its trainer. Because of the bird's success, officers switched the devastating barrage away from the lost battalion. When Cher Ami died one year later, the army transported his stuffed body to the Smithsonian Institution in Washington, D.C., where it is now on display.

Cher Ami alleviated the situation for the trapped men, but they still faced hard fighting. One man lay in a foxhole when a German grenade blew off both his legs. The soldier cried "Mama, Mama, Mama" through a long afternoon, his voice slowly weakening from loss of blood. Finally, he

muttered, "Goodbye, everybody. I forgive all"[99] and died.

Their plight brightened on October 5 when aircraft dropped supplies to the lost battalion. Unfortunately, most of the needed food, water, and ammunition floated outside American lines. McMurtry sent nine men to retrieve whatever they could, but five died and the rest were taken prisoner when they ran into a German patrol. A German officer handed a message to one of the captured, Private Lowell Hollingshead, and returned him to American lines. The message stated that all hope had gone for the surrounded

Carrier pigeons were used to send messages to get supplies back to American soldiers who were in the Argonne Forest.

men and asked them to surrender before they were all killed. Whittlesey and McMurtry refused, believing that help neared and that the Germans would not ask them to surrender unless they suffered also.

The two officers were correct. On October 6 reinforcements broke through to the lost battalion and forced the Germans to draw back. Both Whittlesey and McMurtry received the Congressional Medal of Honor for their bold leadership in the forest.

By the end of the month a series of vigorous American assaults in the Argonne dislodged the Germans, who fell back toward the German border. General Pershing, despite losing many men in the combat and

Premonition of Death

Lieutenant Colonel George S. Patton enjoyed a colorful career, in part because of his actions and partly because of his words. Like General Sir Douglas Haig, Patton believed that destiny controlled one's life. During the fighting in the Argonne, he had a premonition of his own death. He wrote afterward, "Once in the Argonne just before I was wounded I felt a great desire to run, I was trembling with fear when suddenly I thought of my progenitors [ancestors] and seemed to see them in a cloud over the German lines looking at me. I became calm at once and saying aloud 'It is time for another Patton to die' called for volunteers and went forward to what I honestly believed to be certain death."

Patton advanced with six men. Five quickly fell, but Patton and the other survivor continued until Patton felt something smack into his leg. The other man helped Patton into a shell hole, bandaged the wound, and helped save the life of a man destined to be one of the greatest tank commanders twenty-four years later in World War II.

thousands more to an influenza outbreak, ordered his forces to push with more vigor so as to keep the enemy off balance. Rumors of a German request for a cease fire throughout Europe, which would end the fighting, only stiffened Pershing's resolve to deny the enemy a chance to strengthen defenses inside Germany itself.

An End to the Carnage

Following the American success in the Argonne, Germany enacted an orderly withdrawal of forces from the area. Leaving isolated machine gun crews to retard the Americans, according to one correspondent the Germans "backed out as a Western 'bad man' would back out of a saloon with an automatic pistol in each hand."[100]

The bravery displayed by the German soldiers left behind, who had orders to die at their posts, won praise from the Americans. Rarely more than three soldiers at each gun, many of the youthful Germans gave their lives so fellow countrymen could retreat to safety.

American and French troops advanced twenty-four miles along both sides of the Meuse River in November's opening week. Though exhilarated with the rapid progress, every soldier also took extra caution, for they had heard rumors of the war's imminent end. No one wanted to battle through dreary months on the western front only to die days or hours before hostilities terminated. On November 11, the war's final day, Sergeant Rudolph Forderhase, who spoke German, approached two enemy soldiers

manning a machine gun and asked them why they had stopped firing. They replied that they knew the war would be over soon and saw no reason to continue killing.

Though he survived, Lieutenant Francis Jordan was not so fortunate. In what turned out to be the final attack in his sector, on November 11 Jordan was hit by a bullet and knocked on his back. He lay there with German bullets zinging around, then suddenly a stillness covered the battleground. "At 11 o'-clock someone came in to announce that the war was over, but there was little cheering. Someone was able to play a hymn on the pipe organ, however, and somehow they helped us to realize that the war was over."[101]

In the last battle of World War I, twenty-six thousand Allied and German soldiers were killed and ninety-six thousand were wounded.

The Battle of the Meuse-Argonne that helped end the war was the largest ever fought by the U.S. Army. In forty-seven days of constant fighting, twenty-six thousand were killed and ninety-six thousand were wounded out of the more than 1.2 million men who participated. It was a fitting end to a sad affair, a war which sapped Europe of much of its youth and set the foundations of hatred for another, more ghastly, world war twenty years later.

★ Notes ★

Introduction: "Don't Do It Again"

1. Quoted in Martin Gilbert, *The First World War: A Complete History.* New York: Henry Holt, 1994, pp. 224–25.

Chapter 1: The Drive Toward Paris

2. Quoted in Gilbert, *The First World War,* p. 34.
3. Quoted in S. L. A. Marshall, *The American Heritage History of World War I.* New York: American Heritage Publishing, 1964, p. 41.
4. Quoted in Gilbert, *The First World War,* p. 36.
5. Quoted in Jack Wren, *The Great Battles of World War I.* New York: Grosset & Dunlap, 1971, pp. 53–55.
6. Quoted in Gilbert, *The First World War,* p. 36.
7. Quoted in Gilbert, *The First World War,* p. 41.
8. Quoted in Marshall, *The American Heritage History of World War I,* p. 46.
9. Quoted in Gilbert, *The First World War,* p. 57.
10. Quoted in Marshall, *The American Heritage History of World War I,* p. 48.
11. Quoted in Marshall, *The American Heritage History of World War I,* p. 53.
12. Quoted in Wren, *The Great Battles of World War I,* p. 72.
13. Quoted in Gilbert, *The First World War,* p. 70.
14. Quoted in Wren, *The Great Battles of World War I,* p. 76.
15. Quoted in Gilbert, *The First World War,* p. 71.
16. Quoted in Wren, *The Great Battles of World War I,* p. 78.
17. Quoted in Wren, *The Great Battles of World War I,* p. 76.
18. Quoted in Gilbert, *The First World War,* pp. 51–52.

Chapter 2: Gallipoli

19. Quoted in John Keegan, *The First World War.* New York: Vintage Books, 1998, p. 242.
20. Quoted in Gilbert, *The First World War,* p. 147.
21. Quoted in Gilbert, *The First World War,* p. 147.
22. Quoted in Keegan, *The First World War,* pp. 244–45.
23. Quoted in Wren, *The Great Battles of World War I,* p. 156.
24. Quoted in Gilbert, *The First World War,* p. 169.
25. Quoted in Gilbert, *The First World War,* p. 182.
26. Quoted in Gilbert, *The First World*

War, p. 161.

27. Quoted in Gilbert, *The First World War,* p. 190.

28. Quoted in James L. Stokesbury, *A Short History of World War I.* New York: William Morrow, 1981, p. 126.

29. Quoted in Wren, *The Great Battles of World War I,* p. 162.

30. Quoted in Wren, *The Great Battles of World War I,* p. 162.

Chapter 3: Verdun: The Siege of France's Fortress

31. Quoted in Keegan, *The First World War,* p. 278.

32. Quoted in Gilbert, *The First World War,* p. 231.

33. Quoted in http://war1418.com/battleverdun/witness, p. 2.

34. Quoted in Keegan, *The First World War,* p. 281.

35. Quoted in Gilbert, *The First World War,* p. 231.

36. Quoted in Marshall, *The American Heritage History of World War I,* p. 173.

37. Quoted in http://war1418.com/battleverdun/witness, p. 6.

38. Quoted in http://war1418.com/battleverdun/thebattleoftheflanks. p. 6.

39. Quoted in Marshall, *The American Heritage History of World War I,* p. 190.

40. Quoted in Marshall, *The American Heritage History of World War I,* p. 194.

41. Quoted in Marshall, *The American Heritage History of World War I,* p. 192.

42. Quoted in Alistair Horne, *The Price of Glory: Verdun 1916.* New York: Pen-

guin Books, 1993, p. xv.

43. Quoted in Marshall, *The American Heritage History of World War I,* p. 192.

Chapter 4: The Somme: The Slaughter of Britain's Youth

44. Stokesbury, *A Short History of World War I,* p. 148.

45. Quoted in Keegan, *The First World War,* p. 295.

46. Quoted in Keegan, *The First World War,* p. 295.

47. Quoted in Tim Travers, "July 1, 1916: The Reason Why," *MHQ: The Quarterly Journal of Military History,* Summer 1995, p. 65.

48. Quoted in Malcolm Brown, "No-Man's-Land," *MHQ: The Quarterly Journal of Military History,* Summer 1996, pp. 30–31.

49. Quoted in Stokesbury, *A Short History of World War I,* p. 155.

50. Quoted in Wren, *The Great Battles of World War I,* p. 184.

51. Quoted in Wren, *The Great Battles of World War I,* p. 184.

52. Quoted in Robert Cowley, "The Last 140 Days," *MHQ: The Quarterly Journal of Military History,* Summer 1995, p. 74.

Chapter 5: Belleau Wood

53. Quoted in Gary Mead, *The Doughboys: America and the First World War.* New York: Overlook Press, 2000, p. 245.

54. Quoted in Mead, *The Doughboys,* p. 239.

55. Quoted in John Toland, *No Man's Land: 1918, The Last Year of the Great War.* New York: Konecky & Konecky, 1980, pp. 278–79.

56. Quoted in Toland, *No Man's Land*, p. 279.

57. Quoted in Toland, *No Man's Land*, p. 281.

58. Quoted in Toland, *No Man's Land*, p. 281.

59. Quoted in Toland, *No Man's Land*, p. 282.

60. Quoted in Toland, *No Man's Land*, p. 281.

61. Quoted in Allan R. Millett, "Belleau Wood: One Man's Initiation," *MHQ: The Quarterly Journal of Military History*, Autumn 1993, p. 78.

62. Quoted in Millett, "Belleau Wood," p. 78.

63. Quoted in Millett, "Belleau Wood," p. 75.

64. Quoted in Allan R. Millett, *Semper Fidelis: The History of the United States Marine Corps*. New York: Macmillan, 1980, p. 303.

65. Quoted in Millett, *Semper Fidelis*, p. 304.

66. Quoted in Gilbert, *The First World War*, p. 436.

Chapter 6: Saint-Mihiel

67. Quoted in Martin Blumenson, *The Patton Papers, 1885–1940*. Boston: Houghton Mifflin, 1972, pp. 568–69.

68. Quoted in Mead, *The Doughboys*, p. 286.

69. Edward V. Rickenbacker, *Fighting the Flying Circus*. New York: Doubleday, 1965, p. 182.

70. Quoted in Blumenson, *The Patton Papers*, pp. 581–82.

71. Quoted in Clayton D. James, *The Years of MacArthur: Volume 1, 1880–1941*. Boston: Houghton Mifflin, 1970, p. 202.

72. Quoted in Toland, *No Man's Land*, p. 419.

73. Rickenbacker, *Fighting the Flying Circus*, p. 186.

74. Quoted in James, *The Years of MacArthur*, p. 205.

75. Quoted in Nat Brandt, "Sergeant York," *American Heritage*, Vol. 32, No. 5, p. 61.

76. Quoted in Blumenson, *The Patton Papers, 1885–1940*, p. 585.

77. Rickenbacker, *Fighting the Flying Circus*, pp. 190–91.

78. Rickenbacker, *Fighting the Flying Circus*, pp. 188–89.

79. Edward V. Rickenbacker, *Rickenbacker*. Englewood Cliffs, NJ: Prentice-Hall, 1967, p. 124.

80. Rickenbacker, *Rickenbacker*, p. 124.

81. Quoted in Richard O'Connor, *Black Jack Pershing*. New York: Doubleday, 1961, p. 297.

82. Quoted in Marshall, *The American Heritage History of World War I*, p. 346.

Chapter 7: The Siegfried Line: Germany's Last Defense

83. Quoted in Wren, *The Great Battles of World War I*, p. 404.

84. Quoted in Byron Farwell, *Over There: The United States in the Great War, 1917–1918*. New York: W. W. Norton, 1999, p. 223.

85. Quoted in Farwell, *Over There*, p. 218.

86. Quoted in Toland, *No Man's Land,* p. 431.
87. Quoted in Farwell, *Over There,* pp. 224–25.
88. Quoted in Toland, *No Man's Land,* p. 432.
89. Quoted in Marshall, *The American Heritage History of World War I,* p. 334.
90. Quoted in Farwell, *Over There,* p. 224.
91. Quoted in Toland, *No Man's Land,* p. 433.
92. Quoted in Toland, *No Man's Land,* p. 432.
93. Quoted in Mead, *The Doughboys,* p. 311.
94. Marshall, *The American Heritage History of World War I,* p. 335.
95. Quoted in Toland, *No Man's Land,* pp. 466–67.
96. Quoted in Farwell, *Over There,* p. 230.
97. Quoted in Mead, *The Doughboys,* p. 321.
98. Quoted in Toland, *No Man's Land,* p. 468.
99. Quoted in Toland, *No Man's Land,* p. 470.
100. Quoted in Farwell, *Over There,* p. 241.
101. Quoted in Mead, *The Doughboys,* p. 338.

⋆ Chronology of Events ⋆

1914

June 28: Austrian Archduke Franz Ferdinand and his wife are assassinated in Sarajevo, leading most major nations of Europe to declare war.

August 4: Germany invades Belgium.

August 4: France invades Germany.

August 12: 120,000 British soldiers arrive in France.

August 20: German troops enter Brussels.

August 22: Battle of Mons.

August 26: Battle of Tannenberg.

September 2: French government leaves Paris for Bordeaux.

September 5: Battle of the Marne begins.

September 11: Germans pull back from Paris and begin the war in the trenches.

October 11: First Battle of Ypres.

1915

March 18: Allied warships meet disaster in the Dardanelles Strait.

April 22: Germans introduce poison gas.

April 25: British and Anzac troops land on Gallipoli to commence an eight-month campaign to seize the land from Turkey.

May 7: Lusitania is torpedoed by a German U-boat, bringing the United States to the brink of war.

1916

January 9: Final Allied troops are withdrawn from Gallipoli.

February 21: Battle of Verdun begins.

February 25: Germans seize Fort Douaumont.

February 25: General Philippe Pétain assumes command at Verdun.

May 31: Largest naval battle of the war, Jutland, takes place.

July 1: Battle of the Somme begins.

November 18: Battle of the Somme ends.

December 18: Battle of Verdun ends.

1917

January 31: Germany announces the resumption of unrestricted submarine warfare, despite warnings from the U.S. government against such a move.

March 12–15: Russian Revolution overturns the Czarist government for a Communist regime.

April 6: United States declares war on Germany.

June 25: First U.S. soldiers arrive in France.

October 24: Battle of Mons.

November 20: Battle of Caporetto.

1918

June 2: Battle of Château-Thierry.

June 6: Battle of Belleau Wood begins.

September 12: Battle of Saint-Mihiel begins.

September 26: Meuse-Argonne offensive opens.

October 6: Lost battalion is relieved.

October 8: Alvin York awarded the Congressional Medal of Honor.

November 11: World War I ends.

★ For Further Reading ★

Ezra Bowen, *Knights of the Air*. Alexandria, VA: Time-Life Books, 1980. Like most of the books published by Time-Life, this superb account combines exciting narrative with splendid illustrations and photographs. An excellent source for young readers.

Richard Goldstein, *Mine Eyes Have Seen*. New York: Simon and Schuster, 1997. Goldstein gathers first-person accounts of major events in American history. His selections for World War I include Alvin York, Harry S. Truman, the war in the skies, and President Woodrow Wilson.

Gene Gurney, *Flying Aces of World War I*. New York: Random House, 1965. Gurney's choices include eight aces, among them Eddie Rickenbacker. He also provides additional coverage of the air war beyond the exploits of individuals.

Joy Hakim, *An Age of Extremes*. New York: Oxford University Press, 1994. Hakim's acclaimed series includes this volume, which depicts the American entry and involvement in World War I.

Philip J. Haythornthwaite, *Gallipoli 1915*. Oxford: Ospreyg, 1991. The narrative is good, but the maps, pictures, and diagrams accompanying the text make this book more attractive.

Robert Jackson, *Fighter Pilots of World War I*. New York: St. Martin's Press, 1977. Jackson tells the story of fifteen World War I aviators, including American ace Eddie Rickenbacker.

Linda R. Monk, ed., *Ordinary Americans: U.S. History Through the Eyes of Everyday People*. New York: Close Up, 1994. Monk's book, similar to Goldstein's, presents seven accounts of Americans who were involved in the war. The book breathes life into the story by relying on first-person accounts.

Colonel Red Reeder, *The Story of the First World War*. New York: Duell, Sloan and Pearce, 1962. Written by a prolific military historian who specialized in books for the younger market, this volume contains excellent accounts of all aspects of the war.

Earle Rice Jr., *The Battle of Belleau Wood*. San Diego: Lucent Books, 1996. Rice delivers a complete account of the fighting in Belleau Wood. Frequent sidebars and photographs enliven the story.

R. R. Sellman, *The First World War*. New York: Criterion, 1962. Written for the junior high school market, this easy-to-read book delivers an examination of the war that is aimed at beginners.

John B. Severance, *Winston Churchill: Soldier, Statesman, Artist*. New York: Clarion, 1996. This is a fine place to start for anyone desiring to know about the incredible

Churchill. Severance brings him to life and emphasizes the contributions the British leader made before, during, and after World War I.

Gail B. Stewart, *World War I*. San Diego: Lucent Books, 1991. Numerous photos and sidebars supplement a good basic account of the war. The author has written numerous books for the teenage market, and her expertise shows through.

Richard Suskind, *The Battle of Belleau Wood*. London: Collier-Macmillan Limited, 1969. This is one of the best accounts of the marine clash at Belleau Wood. Numerous photographs augment the text.

★ Works Consulted ★

Martin Blumenson, *The Patton Papers, 1885–1940*. Boston: Houghton Mifflin, 1972. Blumenson collects letters written by and to Patton. The section on World War I contains valuable insight into the American effort in France.

Nat Brandt, "Sergeant York," *American Heritage*, Vol. 32, No. 5, pp. 56–64. Alvin York's exploits stir the soul. Brandt's exciting account captures the essence of the humble York and depicts the amazing courage he exhibited.

Malcolm Brown, "No-Man's-Land," *MHQ: The Quarterly Journal of Military History*, Summer 1996, pp. 28–37. This article helps explain the horrors of the zone between opposing sides, commonly known as No-Man's-Land, which played such a crucial role in the war.

Robert Cowley, "The Last 140 Days," *MHQ: The Quarterly Journal of Military History*, Summer 1995. Esteemed historian Cowley examines the Somme's final few months and shows the damage that battle inflicted on nature.

Byron Farwell, *Over There: The United States in the Great War, 1917–1918*. New York: W. W. Norton, 1999. Though an accomplished historian, Farwell does not deliver his best work in this volume. Readers will find the needed basic material but will not be moved by the writing.

Martin Gilbert, *The First World War: A Complete History*. New York: Henry Holt, 1994. Martin, the author of numerous books on war and European history, has written a serious account of the war. He peppers his valuable work with numerous quotes and poems pertaining to the fighting. Though difficult for early teenagers, the book is a wealth of information for the interested reader.

Alistair Horne, *The Price of Glory: Verdun 1916*. New York: Penguin Books, 1993. Horne has written one of military history's classic books with his examination of the important battle of Verdun. His powerful writing vividly conveys the horrors of World War I combat, and he hands the reader a clear picture of Verdun and its impact. If a reader had time for only one book, this would be the choice.

http://war1418.com/battleverdun. The website contains superlative accounts of the fighting around Verdun. The user can focus on first-person narration or head to the general history of the battle.

Clayton D. James, *The Years of MacArthur: Volume 1, 1880–1941*. Boston: Houghton Mifflin, 1970. The first volume in James's multivolume biography of the famous general covers in great detail MacArthur's term in World War I. The smoothly written book is an excellent source of material on the American contribution.

John Keegan, *The First World War*. New York: Vintage Books, 1998. Written by one of the world's foremost military historians, this book offers a thorough explanation of the war. It is one of the top two or three general surveys in print of World War I.

S. L. A. Marshall, *The American Heritage History of World War I*. New York: American Heritage Publishing, 1964. A distinguished military historian, Marshall has written a complete, if not lively, account of the war. What sets this book apart from others are the numerous photographs and the unique maps.

Gary Mead, *The Doughboys: America and the First World War*. New York: Overlook Press, 2000. The author delivers a good account of the United States' role in World War I. He relies upon personal recollections to tell the story.

Allan R. Millett, *Semper Fidelis: The History of the United States Marine Corps*. New York: Macmillan, 1980. One of the premier military historians of our time delivers another fascinating account in this history of the Marine Corps. His chapter on World War I is succinct and smoothly written.

Allan R. Millett, "Belleau Wood: One Man's Initiation," *MHQ: The Quarterly Journal of Military History*, Autumn 1993. Millett writes of the experiences of Gerald C. Thomas, a marine who saw his first action at Belleau Wood.

Richard O'Connor, *Black Jack Pershing*. New York: Doubleday, 1961. O'Connors biography of the famed American officer provides insight into the man and his career. A useful resource.

Robin Prior and Trevor Wilson, *The First World War*. London: Cassell, 1999. Part of a distinguished series of war histories, this book offers a summary of the major battles. Its colorful maps are extremely helpful.

Erich Maria Remarque, *All Quiet on the Western Front*. New York: Fawcett Crest, 1958. The heralded novel has been read by students from around the world since its initial publication in 1928. German author Remarque achieved deserved fame with the antiwar book, which is often required reading in high schools.

Edward V. Rickenbacker, *Fighting the Flying Circus*. New York: Doubleday, 1965. Rickenbacker wrote a compelling account of his experiences battling the enemy over Europe. The reader gains a fascinating glimpse of the dangerous life lived by World War I aviators.

Edward V. Rickenbacker, *Rickenbacker*. Englewood Cliffs, NJ: Prentice-Hall, 1967. Whereas his first book focuses on World War I, this autobiography encompasses Rickenbacker's entire career. The extraordinary man wrote a compelling book.

Siegfried Sassoon, *Memoirs of an Infantry Officer*. New York: Coward, McCann, 1930. Sassoon presents a powerfully written account of war in this memoir of his time in Europe. The book has become a classic.

James L. Stokesbury, *A Short History of World War I*. New York: William Morrow, 1981. Stokesbury, a prolific military historian, delivers a readable, sound account of World War I. Though comparatively brief, the book contains gripping chapters that cover all aspects of the war, both political and military. This book would be an excellent place to start for anyone wanting to learn about the conflict.

John Toland, *No Man's Land: 1918, The Last Year of the Great War*. New York: Konecky & Konecky, 1980. The author of many best-selling history books, Toland turns in another fine account with his moving summary of the war's last year. Toland's heavy emphasis on personal accounts brings the story to life.

Tim Travers, "July 1, 1916: The Reason Why," *MHQ: The Quarterly Journal of Military History*, Summer 1995, pp. 62–73. Travers discusses the horrendous first day of battle at the Somme in a clearly written article.

Jack Wren, *The Great Battles of World War I*. New York: Grosset & Dunlap, 1971. Readers will enjoy the fine mixture of narrative and photographs. Wren is masterly at including quotes from individuals who were present at the key events.

✷ Index ✷

106

★ Picture Credits ★

✫ About the Author ✫

John F. Wukovits is a junior high school teacher and writer from Trenton, Michigan, who specializes in history and biography. In addition to biographies of Anne Frank, Jim Carrey, Stephen King, and Martin Luther King Jr., he has written numerous volumes of military history for Lucent Books, including an account of World War II prisoners of war. A graduate of the University of Notre Dame, Wukovits is the father of three daughters—Amy, Julie, and Karen.